By John Knoepfle

Poems
Twenty Poems of Cesar Vallejo,
     with James Wright and Robert Bly, 1962
Rivers into Islands, 1965
After Gray Days and Other Poems, 1967
Songs for Gail Guidry's Guitar, 1969
The Intricate Land, 1970
Dogs and Cats and Things like That, 1971
Deep Winter Poems, 1972
Our Street Feels Good, 1972
Whetstone, 1972
Thinking of Offerings, Poems 1970-1973, 1975
Poems for the Hours, 1979
A Gathering of Voices, 1979
A Box of Sandalwood: Love Poems, 1979
Tang Dynasty Poems, with Wang Shouyi, 1985
Song Dynasty Poems, with Wang Shouyi, 1985
Selected Poems, 1985
Poems from the Sangamon, 1985
Poems from Tang and Song Dynasties
     (China Edition), 1988
Begging an Amnesty: A Book of Poems, 1994
The Chinkapin Oak, 1995
The One Instant and Forever, 1996.
Prayer Against Famine and Other Irish Poems,
     2004

Prose
Dim Tales, 1989

I Look Around For My Life

An Autobiography by

John Knoepfle

Burning Daylight, an imprint of
Pearn and Associates, Inc.
Colorado

Published by Burning Daylight.
An imprint of Pearn & Associates, Inc., Boulder, Colorado.
For general information about our other products and
services, please contact us at happypoet@hotmail.com
(720) 406-8858.

Cover design by Terence Orin and Steven King at Colorado
Art & Design Company, 502 Sugarloaf Road, Boulder, CO
80302. torin@boulder.net (303) 444-0567.

Edited by Peggy Knoepfle.

Library of Congress Control Number: 2007935132

Knoepfle, John, 1923
I Look Around for My Life, by John Knoepfle. First Edition.
ISBN 978-0-9777318-3-1 (cloth)

For Peggy, as always

Remembering My Family

My very early memories include evenings with my mother and brothers while she darned our socks, and we listened to the radio, the early serials like Molly Goldberg, poor thing. In one episode Molly waited for an old beau who had become prosperous and famous, but he passed her on the stairs and didn't recognize her. He was polite, but he didn't know who she was. My mother would darn our socks at that time. Boys wore knickers then and the socks were knee length. They wore out at the heels. She would darn a pair, roll it up, take the open end and stuff the rest of the rolled up sock into it to make a ball. These she would toss in her willow laundry basket. When our daughter Molly was a toddler, she liked to sit in that basket. It's a little faded now and some strands are missing, but we still stack our laundry in it.

My mother's maiden name was Catherine Cecilia Brickley. Her father had come from Skibbereen in Cork and evidently had done well as a shoemaker on Manhattan's lower East Side. She was a student at St. James, a tough parish school run by the Christian Brothers. Al Smith once carried her school books for her through the Fulton Fish Market on a rainy day. I could never get my mother to talk about her family and only learned why years later. She had lost all but two of her eight siblings, including her favorite sister, before she was a teenager. The year I was born – 1923 – she lost her brother, Cornelius, and her father. I have written about her in *Prayer Against Famine.*

there was the candle christmas eve
after the fasting meal
bees wax and blessed
small tower of ivory
the dark wintry night
for the brickley dead
a little flame and lingering

Four brothers, we were a challenge to my mother, especially because she was pretty much in charge of bringing us up.

and as for myself and my three
brothers
we were the kittiwakes
sheltering in the wounds
of everything she ever loved

We sledded down Halpin Avenue, a 60 degree slope, onto busy Linwood Avenue. I seem to remember a bobsled and my brother Rudy trying to steer it with an ice skate. We had an old Hupmobile. And my brothers found that they could set it with the wheels inside the street car tracks, put it in gear and jump in the back seat. It would then appear to be driving itself down Erie Avenue.

My brother Rudy was the eldest. He graduated from St. Xavier High School when I was still in elementary school at St. Mary's. My father gave him a car as a graduation present. He made a trip to New York and back, and in the fall of that year he entered the Jesuits. Brother Neal didn't survive his sophomore year in high school, but for his purposes it wasn't necessary.

2

He was a salesman of ability. He could sell you your own shirt and you would think you had a bargain. And he had a talent for attracting handsome and lovely girls, though he never married. I remember one of those girls waving to him in tears when he left for the service. My brother Bill earned 12 athletic letters in high school, four each in football, swimming and track. He was co-captain of the football team and had no trouble at all with his academic studies. Bill was impossible to follow, but that's what I had to do.

But I have not mentioned my father. His name was Rudolph Joseph Knoepfle. We called him Pop. He was a film salesman. He would be out every week from Monday until Friday selling movie contracts from big film companies like RKO and Universal Pictures to small town theater owners. His route included part of Indiana, Ohio, Kentucky, some of West Virginia and a little of western Pennsylvania. I have on my grandfather's desk a bronze medal, an eagle mounted on a sunburst. It says, "R. Knoepfle for distinguished sales record from Carl Laemmle, president, Universal Pictures."

My brother Bill went out with my father on one of his weekly journeys. Bill said Pop would go into a small town and meet the theater owner whom he had probably been acquainted with through the years. They would spend the day together trading stories, and maybe he would have dinner with the man and his family. Sometime in the evening, the owner would say, "Well, Rudy, what do you think I should run this year?" Pop would get out his list of films, and they would set up the contract. It could not have been an easy life, logging those miles in the days before air conditioning. And it was not without danger and adventure. Once he was locked in his hotel room by the inn owner in Harlan, Kentucky, because people were shooting it out in the streets.

Pop was of Swiss descent. The family was from the canton of Zurich. My grandfather was a superb wood worker, a skill that he passed on to my uncle Herman and my cousin Stanton. My grandfather's family was just this side of poverty, however. I suspect it was because he was a world class rifle shot, and he competed with the best – including Annie Oakley – at a time when there were no sponsors. You paid for the equipment and the ammunition yourself.

I carried his ashes
on a Monday morning,
my grandfather
who could outshoot
Buffalo Bill.
He gave his pennies to the poor,
the ragged crowd
of my American dream,
when he starved
among his children
in a New York flat.

What little I know of my father's side of the family, I learned from my uncle Augie and my cousin Alma. As for my father, he said that his name was Knoepfle the same as my grandfather and also my great grandfather, very likely. He could speak German, though the Cincinnati

Germans couldn't understand him because it was a Swabian dialect. Pop was very proud of us and once told my mother that I was a "smarta hund." I don't remember what the occasion was, but it was all the German I needed to know.

Getting an Education

From third to eighth grade, I went to St. Mary's Grade School in Hyde Park, Cincinnati. Years later, I met our embattled seventh grade teacher, Sister Veronica. The first thing she said to me was, "I have mellowed." Sister Miriam was our canny eighth grade teacher. She seated us checkerboard fashion – four boys around each girl, four girls around each boy – and she could stare at us in a way that made her look like her eyes were about to pop out. It was her method of scaring us into silence. That was until Bill Christy learned how to pop his eyes back at her, and she could not keep a straight face when he did that. Our eighth grade class of 1937 staged reunions until we were all in our late seventies. Some of our teachers, in their nineties by then, attended. They had led productive lives both here and in Latin America, though Sister Miriam said it was hardly worth it to earn a master's degree, given their scant salaries.

sister miriam's poem

now a dark matter
our perfumed space
polished with light
a woman combing her long hair
beyond existence
beyond our coming and going
where his sandals were
a scent lingering from compassion
the blast of crude nails
cannot change this

the old sister will tell you
martha did her part
she expects you to get the point
figures you are as wise as she is

she will be wrong of course

One of my classmates, Anna Moran, joined the Sisters of Charity and was sent to Peru. After some years of getting around in the Andes on horseback or donkey, she was thrilled when her Order assigned her a jeep. It was due to arrive by ship at the port of Callao, a notoriously rough city on the outskirts of Lima. But then she was faced with bureaucratic obfuscation. The jeep sat in a warehouse. No one would release it. Every week she went to the port office to see if she could get her jeep. It took months, and people got to know her. When she finally drove the jeep out of the warehouse, Callao's dockworkers gave a big cheer for "la monja." Another time she successfully sued a doctor who was cheating his impoverished patients.

How do I know all this? My classmate Tom Linneman has kept the records for our class over the decades. So I know who died at Anzio, who was at Omaha Beach, who was captured, who was cited for courage in Europe, and who served as an Army nurse.

Our old grade school is gone now, leveled for a parking lot. Whatever happened to those huge and dusty pictures of famous poets that lined the walls of our eighth grade class? Edgar Allen Poe was there and John Greenleaf Whit-

tier, Oliver Wendell Holmes, the man who saved
Old Ironsides – and Henry Wadsworth Long-
fellow. It was his translation of *The Divine Com-
edy* that would lead me step by step through
Hell and Purgatory into the light of Paradise –
only to be met by Beatrice, who wanted to know
what kept us so long. And this morning, taped to
my printer, I have the first line of Dante's epic:
"Nel mezzo del camin de nostra vita." How about
that? All that music in that one line. Longfellow
turns up with Whittier again and again in *A
Dictionary of Biblical Tradition in English Litera-
ture.* I meet them there often. Who would have
known? They seemed so ancient and threatening
back in the eighth grade.

Yet the things that struck a chord in me –
the history of the country and of the native peo-
ples – I found outside of school. On cereal boxes,
I read illustrated accounts of the explorers of
North America and of the people they found al-
ready living here. And then there were cards – I
think they came with packs of chewing gum.
They had pictures that I now realize derived
from Catlin's work. I do not remember specific
portraits, except for the picture of Four Bears,
the Mandan chief who died so tragically. These
inspired me to read more books and to walk fur-
rows looking for arrowheads. In time, I discov-
ered the Madisonville site, an agricultural village
and cemetery that was in use between 1000 and
1670 C.E.

Exploring the hills and valleys of eastern
Cincinnati, I had the mandatory encounter with
the Red Bank Road railroad trestle. It was long
and unbelievably high, and you couldn't see a

big steam locomotive coming around the bend behind you until it was on the trestle with you. It's amazing how fast you can run when you're thirteen and leap out of the way at the last minute into a ditch. And the fireman looking at you and laughing his head off.

When I was twelve, I joined Boy Scout Troop 170 at St. Mary's. Until a few years ago, I still had my sash with its thirty-two badges, but it was lost in a move along with my silver eagle. Our troop met in the basement of the church. Since there were no acoustical ceilings for deadening the noise, our weekly volleyball games were ear splitters.

After I returned from the service, I became scout master there for a time. The noise at the games continued unabated and was so emotionally draining that after a volleyball night, I would go with Frank Spaeth and the other assistant leaders and anyone else of age to unwind with several beers at one of the local taverns on Hyde Park Square. Frank, who served with the Marines in World War II, was an able and level-headed scout leader. He later became a Brother of Mary, was a math teacher and high school principal in Walla Walla, Washington, and has been in Hawaii for many years now.

The wonderful old picture magazines, *Life* and *Look*, often published high-quality color spreads of great art. I filled a big scrapbook with these reproductions, including works by Hieronymus Bosch, Matthias Grunewald, Jean Corot and Winslow Homer, to name a few.

I went to high school at St. Xavier High – we called it St. X. It was a streetcar school run by the Jesuits and housed in one of those old nineteenth century buildings covered with pigeons. The yard in front was guarded by a spiked iron fence and faced on Sycamore Avenue in downtown Cincinnati.

As I said before, my task here was to follow in the footsteps of my brother Bill, the star athlete – not to mention my brother Rudy, the Jesuit priest. Somehow I got through it. I was the twelfth man on the eleven-man football squad, a tackle in the days when you could weigh 180 pounds and be a tackle. I charged all the time and was a sucker for the mouse trap. But if the mouse trap didn't work, I was a hero. I remember once breaking up a dull game in the fourth quarter by sacking the quarterback. Not surprisingly, my career was interrupted by things like broken fingers and collar bones and shattered ribs. The upshot of all this was that I was able to earn one letter to match my brother's twelve.

But I did end up president of my class, and it was a class that teachers looked back on with some nostalgia. For instance, in schools like St. X. the freshmen ended up populating the choir and lending their squeaky voices to the (at that time) Latin liturgy. In my senior year the football team got tired of this and joined the choir. Of course, many of us got lost in the middle of the Credo, but we were all tremendous with the Amens. We could blast the stained glass windows out with our Amens.

I should say the football team only had 17 points scored against it that fall. We lost one game by a field goal. The other team had some

Greek kid who came out at the last minute and got it through the uprights. We lost the league championship in the fourth quarter by a touchdown. It was the only score in that game. The other score against us was in the last game we played, and that game ended in a tie. All this came back to me when I was teaching at St. Louis University High School in the early 1960's.

As for my development as a poet, I do remember reading in the eighth grade from Alfred Noyes' "The Highwayman," "One kiss my bonny sweetheart, I'm after a prize tonight." And in high school I entered a speech competition reciting "Jim Bludso of the Prairie Belle" by John Hay. But by my junior and senior years, we had textbooks that did well by us. We got Sandburg's "The fog comes on little cat's feet" and also Yeats. And I would guess it was the Yeats – "Others because you did not keep that deep sworn vow" – that made the difference to me. Although to this day, I can't exactly say how you "Clamour to the heights of sleep."

In our senior year, we read *Macbeth*, including the porter's speech. I understand that in some school districts it was left out – too salacious for the seniors, I guess. We also had Milton's "Allegro" and "Il Pensoroso" and, if I remember, G. K. Chesterton's "The Battle of Lepanto," and Vachel Lindsay's "The Congo."

The spring of my senior year, I arranged the prom, though in the process failed to get a date for myself. As class president, I made the various factions promise not to tear things up, so there was only one bourbon bottle broken in the swimming pool of the country club and only one graduate drove his car over the greens.

Because St. X. was in downtown Cincinnati but drew students from northern Kentucky and the far suburbs of the city, going to a prom or on any kind of date could get complicated. For instance, if you were on a triple date and one girl lived in Hyde Park, another in Fort Thomas and the third on Price Hill, it would take about two hours to pick everybody up and another two to deliver them home.

We graduated in the late spring of 1941. Our Valedictorian turned out to be a prophet of sorts. He predicted that "the Xavier band" would "march forth on oriental sands." On December 7 of that year, the Japanese bombed Pearl Harbor.

Marking Time

After graduation, I went to work for Container Corporation of America, a summer pickup job. I was on the night shift, so I learned what it was to listen for the chatter of birds anticipating sunup. From that experience and also working summer jobs at Heekin Can Company, I got a healthy respect for industrial machinery and for the people who run those machines.

Later in the summer, my high school classmates, Ray Hellman, Joe Bruemmer, Jim Voss and Bob Kipp asked me to go with them on a trip to Clark's Lake, Michigan, just over the border from Ohio – a little lake families liked to visit. When we got there, the landlady rather dubiously rented us a cabin for a week, but we didn't break her house down. We met a bevy of girls from Toledo High School and learned that "blitz in, blitz, blitz out" was a favorite expression of theirs. Perhaps it was something they'd picked up from the news, which was full of the war going on in Europe.

A young fellow, a brother or cousin, I think, accompanied the girls. We ended up playing chess. My Cincinnati friends were impressed that I knew the game. My knowledge was quite rudimentary. I had learned what I knew by playing against my Uncle Augie in Garden City, New York. He had a beautiful board of inlaid wood and finely carved chess pieces. Years later, when I taught at the East St. Louis Residence Center of Southern Illinois University, I organized a chess club there. For all I know, it is still in place at SIU Edwardsville.

After our stay at Clark's Lake, we decided to "go a little further." Going a little further took us to Travers City in northern Michigan, a resort favored by wealthy Catholic families from Cincinnati and St. Louis – the rumor was that marriages were sometimes arranged there. Traveling on to a state park on the Upper Peninsula, we slept out on the ground. In the morning the others threw off their blankets and raced their naked selves into Lake Superior for a dip – and were frozen in various awkward positions. After that, there was no more jumping into the Great Lakes. We contented ourselves by putting our feet into every one of them.

From there it was obvious that we had to go into Canada and then head east for Toronto with a stop off to see the Dionne Quintuplets. They played behind a special glass window, so that visitors could look in to see them but they couldn't see out. They were toddlers by then, old enough to be squabbling among themselves. Canada, we found, was on a war footing – they were rationing gas, and we were cautioned about thieves siphoning off gas tanks. But the people we met were kind and welcoming.

From Toronto we crossed back into the states and returned through northern Ohio to Cleveland where my brother Rudy, now a Jesuit scholastic, taught at St. Ignatius High School. The principal loaned him some money, and Rudy – after turning us loose in the school showers – took us to dinner. In return, we bought a box of very fine cigars for the principal. In those days the Jesuits smoked a lot, and their mothers complained that their cassocks reeked

of tobacco. There was even a ropy stogie man-
ufactured in West Virginia called a "J.F." for
"Jesuit Fathers." You could buy them packed in
a wooden box. I smoked a few myself in my day.

The trip intensified a bonding with my
classmates that did not cease until recent years
when one by one they passed away. Joe Bruem-
mer, who became a diocesan priest, still lives in
Cincinnati, and I give him a call when I come in-
to town.

Among the photos we took, there is one of
me standing next to a historical marker. Below
it, I had written "Father Marquette's death site."
Years later, I lined out a "found poem" from a
letter Marquette wrote to his provincial.

> *marquette in winter camp,*
> *chicago river, 1675*
>
> *I know one of two things*
> *god will break me*
> *because I have been afraid*
> *or he will give me his cross*
> *which I have not borne*
> *since I came to this country*
>
> *the blessed immaculate virgin*
> *will beg this for me*
> *or god will speak my death*
> *and I will stop offending him*
>
> *I try to be ready*
> *putting myself in his hands*
>
> *pray for me and pray god*

will keep me grateful
he has spoiled me always
with so many favors

My work at the Container Corporation had provided me with the money to make the trip and some left over. I used that plus a short-lived football scholarship to enroll that fall at Xavier University. I was on my way.

Then on a mild December evening, I was driving around town with a group of friends when the news came over the radio that Pearl Harbor had been bombed. We were astonished and outraged. I remember we stopped at a gas station, and the attendant told us he wouldn't be there in the morning. He was going to volunteer. Everyone we talked to expected to go into the service. Well, I was already in the ROTC – field artillery, which had never filled me with enthusiasm. You were required to have two years of that. I remember the artillery pieces we had were French 75's, dating from who knows when – World War I maybe. I was more interested in the Navy, so I enlisted. I took an exam and waited for something to happen.

The country was at war. One friend after another left for the service. As far as I can remember, only the pre-med students and the clergy were exempt from the draft. My brother Neal was in the Army, stationed somewhere in the Northwest. Bill, already engaged to his high school sweetheart, Edith Noble, was a bombardier instructor stationed in Florida. But I still hadn't been called up. I finished my freshman

16

year at Xavier, took summer school, and finished my sophomore year.

Somewhere in that time of not knowing what was going to happen next, I took a course in poetry from Father Paul Sweeney. There were stories that he had been a great baseball player and, indeed, he had hands like baseball mitts. He was also a good writer and at one time had a play being considered for production on Broadway, which amused him. "What would I do? Father Sweeney with a play on Broadway!" So he was teaching this class, and he knew how to smoke out writers. He offered a choice between a term paper and an original story or poem. I knew even then that I wanted to be a writer and as any writer knows, if you have a choice between handing in a required essay or writing something that interests you, you take the creative option. I chose to write a narrative poem on Joshua and the battle of Jericho. I don't remember anything about it except for two lines, which convulsed my boozy classmates:

Moses was dead
and on his bier was he.

Shortly after this I became a member of The Mermaid Tavern, a literary society that Father Sweeney sponsored on campus. We all had Elizabethan names. I was Christopher Marlowe. This was a curious foreordaining. The day would come when I would write a Ph.D. dissertation on formulas for praise in Marlowe's work.

Months passed. Except for my friend Tom Clark, who had enlisted in the Air Force, I was the only one of my immediate circle who hadn't been called up. I remember talking on the phone with Tom and being interrupted by a party line busybody who told us we were unpatriotic because we weren't in uniform. I should say that Tom not so long after would be flying cargo planes over Germany. But I also had friends who had been classified 4-F, and it scarred them. A friend of mine, who was a tackle on our high school football team, was rejected because of his eyesight. He never related to any of us after that and when the war ended and we came home, he left town.

John Knoepfle

Navy V-12

I never knew why I wasn't called up immediately. I had been assigned to what was called a V-12 Unit. If you survived that, you would be sent on to Midshipman School. Originally, I was to go to the unit at Western Kentucky University, but then orders came to me and to a number of other recruits from Xavier to report to Hanover, New Hampshire, to the V-12 Unit at Dartmouth College. Our commander was a retired Navy man whose son, we heard, had died in the Straits of Solomon.

On the slow train to Hanover – it took at least two days – I read Stephen Vincent Benet's *John Brown's Body*. What I remember of my arrival at the college is the glorious New England fall with the red maple, the sugar maple, turning. For the first semester I was billeted on the ground floor of Lord Hall. At the Friday forenoon dress parades in front of the dorms, you could hear in the quiet there, interrupted by barked orders, the wailing steam whistle of a distant freight train. It made me feel homesick. That steam train showed up years later in a poem sparked by the sound of a "downgrade diesel" thundering past our house in Edwardsville, Illinois, in about 1959.

> *Those massive locomotives*
> *pulling the heavy strings*
> *lurched under bridges*
> *into utter silence,*
> *then with a whoosh*
> *they clouded the shaken hills.*

19

They were pile driving engines
and they died in my years.
The night is filled with whistles,
like an old freight in New Hampshire
sounding the travail of the race.

With the town overrun by young Navy recruits, Dartmouth parents must have thought it wise to send their daughters somewhere else. In any case, young women were seldom to be seen in Hanover that winter. Our sole entertainment on the weekends was the Nugget Theater. It was always crammed. I remember staring in rapt silence with the rest of the audience at Betty Grable taking a bubble bath. Somebody in the front row stood up and yelled, "How does it look from the balcony?" It brought the house down. But a great disaster occurred. The Nugget burned to the ground one weekend, and the loss of morale was never repaired.

In addition to the courses required by the Navy, such as physics, math and Navy protocol, I was able to take upper division classes in American and English literature. The Navy must have wanted its officers to be literate. I became acquainted with Hawthorne, Melville, Henry James, and Edith Wharton. I also took a creative writing course where I marveled at the sophistication of the other students and listened in amazement to a student from Cape Cod who was speaking an English I had never heard before and could not understand.

We were expected to engage in sports. Since I had boxed at the Fenwick Club when I was a Freshman at Xavier, I did well in the rounds at Dartmouth. We were also taught the opening moves in wrestling, which would stand me in good stead on more than one occasion.

For some reason or other, the neighborhood dogs would join us for breakfast in the cafeteria. The menu was usually a plate of navy beans and corn bread with a dollop of applesauce. But you had to be alert because if you looked away to talk to somebody, you might find a St. Bernard with his head in your plate enjoying your breakfast.

Robert Frost was in residence at Dartmouth that winter, and one Saturday morning I was able to talk with him. When he learned that I was from Cincinnati, he told me about his mother, who lived in central Ohio, and how frightened she was during the Civil War when Morgan's raiders came out of Kentucky to attack Ohio towns.

I am trying to remember what we did that winter in Dartmouth. Yes. The snow. It piled higher and higher so that when you walked from a classroom to the dining hall, you were confined to a canyon and were somewhat fearful that a certain elderly professor whose car was painted white so that he could find it would come roaring up behind you and flatten you into the banked snow on the side of the road. And it was cold, 30 below zero, but a dry cold and not as chilling as the raw, wet cold in Cincinnati.

And there were weekends with shore leave when we traveled around New England having various unremarkable adventures. I learned, for instance, that the girls at Wellesley had sturdy legs from walking to classes on their hilly campus.

On one occasion, somewhere in rural Vermont, we had calculated that we could get back to Dartmouth on the Sunday train only to learn at the local station that there was no Sunday train. While we were contemplating the consequences of being AWOL, a slow freight came to the crossing. We ran out and stormed onto the caboose – two fore and two aft. Once the brakeman had recovered, he let us read the caboose comic books. When we passed through a town, we had to duck below the windows, and before we entered the yards at White River Junction, he stopped the train so that we could cross through the woods and take the road back to Hanover.

We took part in the usual collegiate high jinks, though ours look pretty innocent by today's standards. We read the war news, listened to it in the evening on the radio, heard and discussed the rumors that filtered through the V-12. But we were not subjected to the 24-hour media blast that people get today. At the same time, we lived this life. We weren't in combat; we weren't overseas, though we knew that very shortly we would be. We had no idea where we were going or what we would be doing.

I remember when I came home for a while that summer. I was in uniform and went to the Moonlight Gardens at Cincinnati's Coney Island. I saw my old friend Jack Hoenemeyer on the dance floor – he had been captain of the St. X. football team. He was also in uniform, a sergeant in the Army. We were glad to see each other. He would be captured at Normandy and survive a

German prison camp. But that night was just our night.

Back at Dartmouth, I remember being very busy doing math and physics problems in the top floor center room of Middle Massachusetts Hall. A friend in the V-12 told me later that everyone thought I was very studious and dedicated. I was just trying to get through. I wasn't sure I could pass the courses.

When I see Dartmouth in my mind's eye, it is toward early evening in a yellow haze as the lights come on. I remember many of the lines in "Glory to Dartmouth" and the more questionable "Dartmouth's in Town Again." And odd pieces of information – how in the distant past, for instance, students had been expelled for singing "On the Road to Mandalay." It was "wasting Christian kisses on a heathen idol's foot" that did the students in. And there were the ghosts of poets past in the drinking songs. I also found in my library this morning a handsomely printed small book called, *The Arts Anthology: Dartmouth Verse, 1925*, printed in Portland Maine by the Mosher Press, with a preface by Robert Frost:

> *No one is asking to see poetry regularized in courses and directed by coaches like sociology and football. It must remain a theft to retain its savor. But it does seem as if it could be a little more connived at than it is. I for one should be in favor of the colleges setting the expectation of poetry forward a few years (the way the clocks are set forward in*

May), so as to get the young poets started earlier in the morning before the freshness dries off. Just setting the expectation of poetry forward might be all that was needed to give us our proportioned number of poets to Congressmen.

John Knoepfle

From Whaleboats to LCVPs

That summer of 1944, the Navy sent me to Camp MacDonough on Lake Champlain at Plattsburgh, New York. This was part of the Navy's plan to commission many officers to staff the unprecedented number of landing crafts and all manner of ships being built for the invasions of Italy, Normandy, the Pacific Islands and Japan. I think the Navy anticipated that the casualties would be heavy and many ships lost. I liked Plattsburgh because we were out on the water. We had a congenial officer over us, Ensign Peckinpaugh. At the end of our tenure there, we chipped in and bought him a sword.

The time there was physical. We manhandled oars in whaleboat races on Lake Champlain. Yes, these were genuine whaleboats, five or six oars to a side and very heavy. We got more training in wrestling. I was picked to oppose a burly Italian fellow, who had been the catcher for the Yale baseball team. My friends winced – they thought I would be destroyed. As it turned out, I had learned some skills in the wrestling class at Dartmouth. There, I always lost to the person I was teamed with, but my experience stood me in good stead here. I threw the Yale catcher three times in three minutes – he just didn't know the opening moves. Fortunately I did not have to face him in the boxing tournament. He was a terror in the ring, and I had already lost a decision in the quarter finals, a decision that was heartily booed – the best way to lose a match.

25

Our company was a spirited group. Making myself useful, I wrote our marching song to the tune of "McNamara's Band." I remember a few of the lines.

> *We have coral-covered shoulder*
>   *boards*
> *and salt behind the ears.*
> *Our hair is made of seaweed*
> *and it's stowed away in tiers.*

"Tiers" is a technical term in the Navy – it has to do with the way the lengths of anchor chain are stored one on top of the other. There was a chorus of sorts:

> *All the fellows down in Washington*
> *who know their ensigns best*
> *they choose the men from*
>   *Company D*
> *before they choose the rest.*

The class in naval gunnery was formidable. You had to master several mathematical equations that enabled you to calculate the distance you had to fire and at the same time the ship's roll and other variables. A young lieutenant greeted us the first day with these words: "I am your instructor. It is true that I have a master's degree, but it is in agriculture." He solved this problem by having the good mathematicians in the class dope out the equations and then explain them to the rest of us. Thus I passed the course in gunnery and became a small boat officer on an attack transport. And I have to say here that I loved the sea. But I think in candor that the good mathematicians who figured out the gunnery problems ended up on the quarterdecks of cruisers and destroyers.

After Plattsburg, the Navy sent me to San Diego where I joined a unit in the amphibious fleet. We practiced landings and troop transfer on the beach that fronts the old Coronado Hotel. It's odd what you remember. I learned that Marilyn Boyd, my next door neighbor on Pape Avenue in Cincinnati, was in the WAVES. We had dinner together at a San Diego hotel with John Ulmer, who had been her classmate at Withrow High School and who was a fellow ensign in my outfit.

In mock assault landings, we practiced hitting the beaches and pulling out. Working with the crew of the attack transport that we would pick up later, we came alongside other transports anchored off the beach and boarded them by way of the cargo nets hung over the side for our practice. We then spidered our way back down to our boats, which were known as LCVPs – landing craft vehicle personnel carriers.

On one particular day, a blue sky windy morning. I remember telling the men who had false teeth to put them in their pockets before we set out. I must have been clued into this by more experienced officers. But the men were proud and didn't follow my advice. Well, we practiced the landings and it was glorious, roaring into the beach on a high surf and then pulling out again. My crew proved itself wonderfully seaworthy, but then about noon we anchored out off the shore and "nested" groups of boats at anchor – tying them together and letting them rock in the sea. I don't know what we were given to eat, but I know that the drink was some kind of Kool-aid that would make you sick under the best of circumstances. It wasn't a minute or two before men were upchucking over the sides of the boat, and one or two lost their teeth.

We finished our training, and the whole crew went by rail up the coast to Astoria, Oregon. I remember miles of orange groves and snow-capped Mount Shasta. As we approached the Oregon border, some Army photographers rushed into the men's room in order to piss on California. They must not have been happy campers there.

When we got to Portland, it was early evening, and our train sat out in the railroad yards. This was our last night before putting out to sea. By morning we'd be headed for Astoria where we would board ship. It didn't seem possible to keep the men cooped up in the train, so the word came down from the higher ups in the command to the crew officers that we were not to notice any crew members we might meet wandering around town. The word must have also gone out to the shore patrol because nobody in our crew was arrested that night.

John Knoepfle

In the Pacific

I reported October 18, 1944, at 1350 a-
board the USS Deuel. It was an attack trans-
port, essentially a cargo ship that had been fit-
ted to carry a brace of LCTs – landing craft
capable of carrying tanks – and some 16 LCVPs,
the boats I had trained on in San Diego. The
LCVPs could carry 36 combat troops. They were
flat-bottomed boats without much of a draft,
which made them skittish on high waves.

Incidentally, the Deuel had a history be-
yond World War II. The ship was returned to
service in the Korean War, and members of the
crew that served her in that conflict maintain a
website. Like other ships in that class, the Deuel
was named after a county – Deuel County – in
the state of Nebraska.

It was a gray, wet morning in Astoria when
we picked up the Deuel and put out to sea. We
crossed the Desdemona Sand Spit through
patches of fog and cries of gulls and the warning
of the bell buoy. It is a memory that has stayed
with me, and I used it years later in a poem
about Gandhi – how he began this movement of
nonviolence and how it was like leaving the
safety of the shore for a vast, unexplored ocean:

> *calling us out of ourselves*
> *far from justice to that moment*
> *with no bearings no fixed point*
> *only the bell buoy*
> *slipped from its moorings*
> *clanging in the drift of the sea*

We steamed north up the coast and on an incredibly beautiful morning made our way up through the Juan de Fuca Strait to Bremerton, Washington. The ship was put through its sea trials there, and we came back out to sea and caught our first storm, which caused some damage. Already we were experienced sailors, you could say.

Our destination was Honolulu. At the docks at Pearl Harbor, the layer of congealed grease and oil still floating on the water was over a foot thick. While we waited to pick up the rest of the fleet, we did massive invasion exercises.

Something else happened that I have trouble believing even to this day. While I was on the island, a friend looked me up – he was with an intelligence unit. We spent an afternoon touring the mountains and admiring the scenery. Along the way, we stopped at some bars and refreshed ourselves. At one point I wanted to know what was in the leather pouch on the back seat of our jeep. "Oh, that's the battle plans," he replied, "for Iwo Jima."

My job as an ensign in the Amphibious Corps was to bring combat troops into hostile beaches and to supply them and carry the wounded out. But when I came aboard the Deuel, I wanted to understand how the ship was rigged, so I had a number of books on seamanship, including books on the rigging for cargo ships. I studied those, and this enabled me to have one small triumph that I have cherished ever since.

I had been standing watch in the night – that was at Hilo – and after I was relieved of duty, I went topside and found a lieutenant berating several crestfallen ensigns to the amusement of some of the crew. He was a ship's carpenter who had come up through the ranks to gain his commission. Suddenly he pointed up into the rigging – "You dumb 90-day wonders, you wouldn't know a double-luff if it fell on you."

I looked up where he was pointing and I said, "Well, for an old sea dog like you that may be a double-luff, but to a 90-day wonder like myself, it looks more like a two-fold purchase."

He peered up into the dark and said, "My God, you're right."

For a few days, I was a folk hero among the other ensigns.

On New Year's Day, 1945, we picked up an Army unit and steamed west into the Pacific. I'm not sure where we disembarked the troops, but I know we were at Eniwetok in the Marshall Islands. It was dark, and we were inside the atoll.

But let me tell you about being at sea. There was a night when the moon was full, and it beamed through a scattering of clouds so that the Pacific in its restlessness was filled with lakes of silver. We went to the ship rails to watch it. It was so remarkable that you were surfeited with it and had to leave it and go back to your quarters. In a poem called "On a Fall Night," I wrote of the moon from that shipboard memory:

Dropping one by one her silver combs
Into the wise and secretive Pacific.

Where did we pick up the 5th Marines? I think it was during a massive transfer of personnel in the seaway defined by the islands of Saipan, Tinian and Guam. On Guam I remember these huge toads, ten times bigger than any I had seen in the States – it's odd what the mind retains. But we must have picked up the 5th Marines there in that seaway.

Early that morning we put the boats over the side of the ship. They were hung from a pair of steel cables suspended from davits. In order to keep the cables steady as our boat was let down, our boatswain had attached a line between the two cable hooks. But our boat hit the sea at the crest of a swell. When the wave gave out, the boat dropped, and the cross line of the cables caught the starboard machine gun housing and hurled it about forty feet into the sea. Fortunately, we hadn't come aboard or someone might have been sliced in two – most likely myself since I would have been standing in front of the starboard machine gun housing.

It was a warm day. When we embarked the Marines, I told them to put on their helmets, but many of them did not. The sea was running high and when we turned into the fairway, we crested a heavy swell. The steel window in the bow of the LCVP caved in and struck some of the men in the back. After that I had no problem with helmets.

When we transferred personnel to attack transports, the transports would anchor athwart the swells so that you could bring your boat in to calmer waters on the lee side of the vessel. Practicing this back in San Diego, we had a calm sea and it was positively enjoyable – the troops clambering up the rope nets hung over the side of the transport. But here the swells were eight feet high. If you tried to get on the net when you were at the bottom of a swell, the boat coming up could crush you against the ship's side.

We told the troops to leave their rifles and their gear with us and to line up four at a time and be ready – and when we hit the crest of a swell, I'd say, "Now!" They leaped, caught the lines and muscled their way up the net. After the last man had boarded the ship, we gathered all the gear and had it hauled topside. We cast off our lines then and drifted into the fairway. I told our coxswain to set our course in a wide lazy circle, and we rested, sprawled in the hold of the LCVP with cigarettes dangling from our mouths. By some miracle, we found our way back to our mother ship.

I have met veterans since then who were among the troops being transferred that day. They said it was a terrifying experience and that there were casualties.

The 5th Marines were to experience their first combat when we brought them to that troublesome beach at Iwo Jima.

Iwo

I should make a digression here to speak of our collection of phonograph records. We had *Oklahoma* – "Poor Judd is dead. A candle lights his head." And a single with "Me and Brother Bill Went Hunting" on it. And I remember another record. Its lyrics, "Give me your smile, the sunshine of your eyes, earth could not hold a fairer paradise" made us sick for romance that none of us had ever had or would have, I imagine. A more cynical seventy-eight warned:

> *When you're cheatin' on your baby,*
> *did you think that maybe*
> *your baby may be cheatin' on you?*
>
> *And if you're foolin' 'round*
>   *somebody,*
> *did you think somebody*
> *may be foolin' 'round your baby*
>   *too?*

We played these records over and over. I have inflicted "When you're cheating on your baby" on friends and family all the years since.

There were three of us in our quarters, a small room with double bunks on each side and a port hole. We couldn't use the starboard upper bunk because of the heavy wiring so close overhead. My roommates were Ensign Johnson and Ensign Nay. We always called Johnson "Swede," though as a matter of fact he was Norwegian. I didn't know until quite recently that his first name was Alfonse. Ensign Nay was in charge of the two LCTs we carried – Landing Craft Tanks. They were larger and sturdier than our LCVPs – Landing Craft Vehicle Personnel.

I have lost touch with everyone, even my old friend John Ulmer. He was called back into service and injured at sea during the Korean War. Later he moved away from Cincinnati, I think. I had a letter from Swede after the war. He had married and become a Lutheran pastor somewhere in the Dakotas. And one other fellow officer, whose name I forget now, was also from Cincinnati. We once had a beer together at a bar on Eastern Avenue, but he was very uneasy because his wife wouldn't have approved of that.

It is almost due north from the Marianas to Iwo Jima. Our convoy, protected by destroyers and destroyer escorts, was part of the Fifth Fleet. Our ship had a comfortable roll. A destroyer escort was something else. On a windy day, you could see the keel half out of the water, lurching up over a swell and then crashing down. You wondered how the crew could have taken that pounding. On February 19, 1945, we were off the island of Iwo Jima. The landings began early that morning.

I was a boat officer. A boat officer was in command of a wave of eight or ten LCVPs, each carrying 36 combat troops – the Fifth Marines in this case. I sat on the engine housing in the stern. It was important to keep the lines of boats straight so that each wave would hit the beach at the same time. To do that we used hand signals. The night before, each of the boat officers had been given a radio to let the naval command know that we had made our landing.

35

But we only had one instruction session on how to use those radios. The truth is I didn't know if any of my radio messages got through, and I have a suspicion the others didn't either.

We had to discharge the troops and get off the beach before the next wave came in, but as it turned out, the beach itself was cluttered with boats that were broadside on the sand – there was a powerful cross current along the beach there that hadn't been calculated. Of course, there were patrol boats trying to get these stranded LCVPs back out to sea.

When we dropped our ramp, the Marines hesitated suddenly, and I must have said, "Good luck." Then they hit the beach.

Two years ago I was asked to speak about the war. I was reading from some notes I had made – and when I came to that moment when I had said, "Good luck," it almost demolished me. I had not spoken of that in over sixty years.

I should say that the Japanese strategy was to allow the first waves of Marines in unopposed in the morning and then to cut off the later waves in the afternoon, trapping the first arrivals. When we went in at two in the afternoon, the enemy firing was well underway. I heard a shell whistle overhead, though I did not see it. But Swede, who was commanding the wave behind us, he saw it. The shell hit in the water just off our fantail. He told me later that he almost had a heart attack. In any case, we got our boats safely back to the Deuel.

Our ship was also a hospital ship, carrying a complement of doctors, corpsmen, and medical supplies. In addition to bringing the troops to the beach, we brought the wounded back, though I was never called upon to do this. Our medical team took care of the wounded. But of those who were returned to the ship, some died, and they were buried at sea.

If I remember right, by the evening after the landing the beach had been pretty well cleared of stranded and battered boats and equipment. The fighting had gone inland by then, and we couldn't see anyone on the beach. I was ordered to carry some ammunition conveyors to the Marines. The conveyors were long and came in sections. Before they could be lowered into our boat, they were assembled on deck and bound together with heavy steel cables. It was dark when we dropped into the sea and took our cargo on.

The surf was high when we reached the beach and released the ramp. We came in on the port side of an LST. I still remember seeing high above us the port forward gunner with his 40 millimeter trained on Suribachi Yama. He was watching for any flashes of light from the mountainside, and we could see the undersides of his eyes. He never looked down.

The sea swamped our fantail as we tried to pull the conveyors out of our boat. But they were strapped together as a single unit. We couldn't sever the steel cables, and the load was too heavy to drag onto the beach. At one point we managed to raise it up about a foot, but had to drop it again – it landed on my toe. Finally, we put the ramp up and backed into the sea.

I don't know how we managed this because once we were off the beach, our engines died and we drifted north under Suribachi Yama. We were exhausted. I have a memory of our coxswain – his name was Kelly – singing "When Irish Eyes are Smiling," but I wouldn't swear by this. We were drifting into the open sea north of the island. Luckily, we were spotted by a patrol boat out picking up strays. They threw us a line and towed us to a pool of LCVPs moving in a slow circle.

It was on February 23 that the famous flag raising took place on Suribachi Yama. We could see it, a dot on the rim of that volcanic peak. It was a moment of exhilaration throughout the whole fleet. That same night there was an air raid alert, and the ships opened up. It was a spectacular display, the big guns from battle-ships, cruisers, destroyers, and the amphibious fleet blasting the dark sky.

Our ship was not firing. There seemed to be some question whether there were planes up there or not. But we were at battle stations, and I was in charge of the forward starboard gun crew. We were waiting for orders to fire and looking up at all that ordinance exploding in the sky. I said, "Some of that has got to come down." And then one did.

It was a shell, possibly a 20 millimeter that explodes on contact. It landed between the two gun crews, and the shrapnel hit everybody. For the most part the injuries were superficial, except for what happened to me.

When the shrapnel struck the back of my legs, I passed out. When I came to, I was the only one there, and I thought my crew had all been killed. To this day, I don't know where they went, but I guess they had assumed that I was dead. In any case, I managed to go aft under the bridge yelling for a corpsman, and then I passed out again.

I woke up on a table in the wardroom. The medics were cutting off my blood-soaked hightops. They managed to stabilize the bleeding, and I got back to my sleeping quarters to spend the rest of the night vomiting into a bucket there.

The right leg healed quickly, but it took me a good five weeks to be able to walk without my left leg buckling under me. I walked back and forth under the bridge and in time got so that I felt all right.

While I was recuperating, I sometimes chatted with other injured personnel. I remember an Air Force captain, who told me he had the worst case of athlete's foot in the Navy. He said that when he was returning from a sortie to land on Iwo, the entire wing under his command was shot down by friendly fire. He had no intention of going back up again.

By the time I resumed ship's duties, we had returned to the Marianas to drop off the wounded. From the Marianas, we went to the Solomon Islands. As we passed through the Straits of Solomon on a beautiful Sunday morning, there was a profound silence aboard our ship and all the other ships in our convoy. This was where so many ships had been lost in defense of Guadalcanal. A holy place.

Down Solomon

Ten days and south from Iwo,
a sea that calm you could have
  walked it
tiding the rare Solomons.
We knew the dead it held
were our own dead
and gave them silence under Savo.

That evening we anchored off Florida Is-
land, and the scent of the tropical flowers made
us all homesick.

Near the shadowy island
we made a wall for our war.
with rambler rose and the lilac.

The gray dawn touched us,
and these were put away.

We saw a temple on the mountain,
all in rubble,
washed in a blue wind.

And some of us stayed there forever
with the rambler rose, the lilac,
the blue keen wind.

John Knoepfle

I should say we crossed the equator on this voyage. My injury spared me some of the traditional harassment. All I had to do was kiss the belly of King Neptune. We went south then to Espiritu Santo in the New Hebrides east of Australia, where we picked up the Army's 27th. They were coming to support the 7th Marines in the invasion of Okinawa.

Okinawa

The 27th Infantry, I think, were weary troops. We were told they had been in the Pacific too long. For the Okinawa invasion, they had been assigned to a new commander – General Simon Bolivar Buckner, Jr., the son of the confederate general who surrendered Fort Donaldson to Grant in 1862. Our convoy steamed north for Okinawa.

Strange things linger in the memory. There was a Catholic chaplain with the 27th – Swede liked the sermon he gave. This chaplain was hearing everyone's confession, at least all the Catholic troops. He had a five dollar bill, and he said that anyone who could confess a sin that he hadn't heard before, he would give them the five dollars. Evidently, no one was able to collect.

When it came time to assault the beach, it was determined that the LCVPs couldn't get over the coral formations there, so Army DUKWs were used. A DUKW was an amphibious version of a heavy cargo truck with a big pair of wheels in the back. The odd name was a military code for these features. We called them "ducks" because they could go on water and come up on the land. As this was a naval operation, the boat officers had to accompany the assault waves of DUKWs. So we went in.

But when our unit got the DUKW up on the beach, no one had any idea where we were or where we were supposed to go. We ended up, myself, the corporal and some other soldiers, driving around all night, looking for the command we were supposed to report to.

At one point we entered a village. It was hard to see anything, and we thought it might be a good idea to get out of there. The corporal started to make a turn, and we found ourselves staring into a thatched dwelling of some kind, hoping no one in that darkness was pointing a machine gun at us. But the house was empty. The villagers had fled our bombardment, and the Japanese had decided not defend the beach areas. They were holed up in well-fortified positions in the high country further inland.

Morning found us in wide valleys where great ancestral tombs were maintained on the hillsides. We finally located the beach headquarters. When you try to remember things after so many years, you lose connections. I don't recall when I left the Army unit and the DUKW. I just remember standing in a wooded area and staring at the body of a woman in black silks, sprawled face down on the path in front of me. Her silk dress had hitched up over the back of her knees, and her legs were already swollen and somewhat discolored. One arm was extended in front of her, her fingers reaching for the small clay pot that had scattered some beans on the path there. I have carried that image with me for more than sixty years. An Army chaplain happened by, and I asked him what would happen to her. He said the bulldozer would come and put her under.

Aboard ship again, nobody seemed to be interested in my adventures. I resumed normal ship's duties, but at some point during the next several days, I noticed that the back of my left leg was swollen and when I felt it, it was pulsing.

43

So I went and asked one of the ship's doctors what he made of this. He examined me and told me I had an aneurism. He said that instead of knitting back artery to artery and vein to vein, the main artery and the vein had knitted together, thus the pulse – and that I could die at any time. "Well, in that case," I said, "I should be relieved of ship's duty."

Then the doctor invited all the medical corpsmen to come and listen with the stethoscope, and they said things like "Oh boy." The doctor told me to keep an elastic bandage wrapped around the knee to protect it.

I remember we saw a kamikaze hit one of our transports in the harbor there at Okinawa. Years later, I learned from a colleague at the University of Illinois Springfield that his father had been a deck officer aboard that ship and had survived the attack. At Iwo, the kamikazes were not in evidence, but at Okinawa they wreaked havoc on the destroyers and destroyer escorts on picket duty north of the island.

John Knoepfle

Looking for a Surgeon

We sailed along the west coast of the Philippines to the port city of Alonggapo, north of Manila, and I was transferred to a hospital LST. The hold had been converted to a ward for the wounded. It was a cruddy ship. I guess the crew had been out to sea too long and were under a lot of strain.

One of the wounded there was a young black sailor. In those days the Navy did not allow African Americans to serve except as cooks and stewards – Harry S. Truman put an end to that later when he became President. The young sailor was angry. He told me with incredulity in his voice that the officers aboard his ship wanted to see him dance. His father owned two pharmacies in Chicago.

I was put ashore at Manila, which had been devastated by attacks and counterattacks, and then flown to an ancient town on the eastern seaboard. I remember a church there with massive carved wooden doors and the local people coming to the Army mess hall for handouts of food and used coffee grounds.

From there, I was flown to New Guinea where I drowsily woke up for a moment. There was really no place for the wounded on our plane. We were drugged with morphine and slept on the mail bags. The next stop was the island of Manus in the Admiralties. Manus was the tropical paradise that you see in South Pacific movies. Societies of huge bats lived in the palm trees, however, something the movies had overlooked. As it turned out, the doctor who could have operated on my leg had already left that lovely island.

We had an air raid on Manus. It is hard to imagine that the Japanese could mount one that far south at that time in the war, but they did. Although there was some minor damage, no one was injured.

Those of us recovering from wounds or waiting for an operation went from one day to next, enjoying the atmosphere. I remember a movie we saw, a documentary about Alaskan glaciers featuring the Jesuit priest Father Hubbard. It was the only time I saw troops applaud a movie. I don't know if it was because of the scenery in Alaska or because they admired Hubbard's achievements and his style.

I met a Navy nurse there, who was from northern Kentucky. When I got home, I called her family and told them she was doing well. I also called the family of a steward I knew on the USS Deuel who was from Cincinnati. Then I contacted John Ulmer's aunts to tell them he was well. They were so proud of him they could hardly speak.

John Knoepfle

Sentimental Journeys

In time, I was shipped back to the states aboard the USS Talamanca, a luxury liner that had been commissioned to the Navy. It had teakwood decks. There was a moment aboard the Talamanca when I went topside and saw a large number of officers stretched on the deck there, airing out their dress uniforms and getting the Pacific tan. I was surprised. I couldn't think of one person in the Pacific fleet who was interested in a tan when the sun was beating down on us and we were wearing hats and long sleeved shirts to protect ourselves.

It was a gray morning when we came to port under the Golden Gate Bridge. A band played us ashore, and at the hospital the base commander saw to it that we were treated wonderfully. What do I remember? I remember one evening sitting in a quiet bar on one of San Francisco's hills. I was by myself, and then this lovely voice floated from the jukebox:

I'm gonna take a sentimental journey,
Gonna set my heart at ease.

There was no one in San Francisco who could operate on me either, so I was ordered to the Great Lakes Naval Base, north of Chicago. It was at the end of July when I got on the train, which was filled with returning veterans. It was a three-day journey across the country. The train would come to a stop alongside the local depot in a small town, and a man we had been sitting with for hours would get up and straight-

47

en his tie and smooth down his uniform. And when you looked out the train window, you would see a young woman waiting there, dressed in a summer frock, a small wind blowing her skirt, and a toddler or two at her side. And then you saw the embrace. It left you heavy in your own heart. That lucky veteran had completed his sentimental journey, but I was going to a new life that I knew nothing at all about.

On August 6, 1945, the bomb was dropped on Hiroshima. I was at the naval hospital recuperating from the operation which had repaired my leg. I let the newspaper drop beside me on the hospital bed. I was sickened to read the news. Now after all these years, I think the bishops of Nagasaki said the first and last words about the bombings: "The victims were the lambs who were sacrificed to end the war."

When I was sufficiently recovered, I was given leave and came home. I knew I was returning to see Pop for the last time. I had learned before Okinawa that he was seriously ill. He was suffering from lung cancer and had only a few weeks to live. For many months my mother had taken care of him, pretty much by herself. After I came home, whenever he saw me around the house, he would think he was seeing me for the first time back from the service. "Oh there's John," he would say, overjoyed once again.

But the morning came when I heard my mother scream. I hurried down the stairs and found her holding him in her arms and rocking him. He was scarcely more than bones in his skin. Cora Grundy, the woman who had helped my mother for years with the washing and ironing, was there. When we laid Pop out on his bed, she closed his eyes and bound his jaw shut.

I have to say something here about Cora. I don't remember when she was not with us. She spent her career doing washing and ironing for a small number of families in Cincinnati. Cora's mother had been a slave on one of the plantations in Kentucky. She never spoke of it and I do not know how I learned this – perhaps from my mother. Cora lived on Eastern Avenue and I would guess now that she outlived most of the women she worked for. She always liked me to drive her home, rather than brother Neal. Neal was what might be called a casual driver, and Cora would be afraid for her life. After the war, the families she worked for banded together and paid for her Social Security.

After my father died, my mother told me that when the newsboys came through the neighborhood calling out that President Roosevelt had died, my father, dying himself, heard it and burst into tears. Pop became a Catholic late in his life. According to the priest who instructed him, his questions were pointed and challenging. He was buried from St. Mary's in Hyde Park.

Retrieving an Education

I won't try to explain this, but there was some question about my status in the Navy. The Great Lakes doctors were arguing with the Navy doctors in Washington, D.C., about whether I was fit for duty. Each time a letter went from Great Lakes to D.C., I asked for and was given a thirty-day leave. This went on for two years.

I used those leaves to return to Cincinnati and take more classes. I finished my bachelor's degree in philosophy at Xavier and also a master's degree in English. I began to write again and to learn how to put a poem together.

My master's thesis was an "Oratorio for Advent and Christmas." It was published in the 1947 *Xavier Athenaeum*, the school literary magazine. It begins with a prologue, moves to the Annunciation and ends with a shepherd's chorus as they come to adore the Christ Child.

It was my first attempt at an extended work. I knew that W. H. Auden had written an oratorio, and I consulted with a musician and learned that oratorios are composed with different voices, points of view and styles. Just to catch the flavor of my attempt, I'll quote from "One Alone: Recitation:"

> *O Mystery, who am I, what am I,*
> *To penetrate the fastness of your love?*
> *I have run a path of silver steps*
> *Thinking I have found you;*
> *Now they vanish here*
> *On the ridge of a sun burnt hill.*

John Knoepfle

My oratorio was staged at Mount St. Joseph's College in Cincinnati, but I didn't see it because I had already moved to Washington, D.C. I have a faint remembrance of meeting the girl who played the part of God.

There were some interesting themes and images in that oratorio, but I did not relate them to my own time and place. In that respect, Auden was way ahead of me. His oratorio was infused with the politics of his day, just as the medieval drama, *The Second Shepherd's Play*, is full of the theology of its day along with the lore and speech of shepherds. At that stage in my writing, I wasn't able to make that fusion.

Catholic University

I was restless and unsettled at home and decided to enroll at Catholic University in Washington, D.C. In addition to a small disability payment, I still had the G.I. Bill, so I drove to CU, got a room in the dorm and enrolled in graduate studies in English. Except that I knew I wanted to write, I had no clear idea of why I was doing this. Worse yet, I was ill-prepared for the classes. I can tell you that trying to read *The Faerie Queen* on a winter night in the dorm was like having a hand slowly clutching your heart. I worried about the course work and about the trouble I was having deciding what to do with my life. It wasn't long before I was suffering from a severe depression.

One Sunday late in the semester, I went to the cafeteria to have supper. Someone at the head of the line was being turned away by the cashier because he wasn't a CU student. He saw me and said "I know him." It turned out he was an old acquaintance from Xavier, and we ended up eating together.

I hadn't talked to him more than five minutes before he knew what was troubling me. He directed me to a priest in the Dominican House, a scholar of some reputation. I visited this priest and in the course of our conversation told him, "Father, at this point in my life if I was asked to go to China, I would drop everything and do it."

He replied, "You have all your books packed to study over the Christmas holidays, don't you? Leave them at the university. Go home and

52

have a good time. The world is full of happy people who flunked out of graduate school."

Then he addressed my real problem: "You don't have a vocation; you have a fear of having a vocation. And because you're projecting this, other people are pushing you in this matter. The next time someone does this, ask them if *they* have a vocation."

Back in Cincinnati, I soon had a chance to test this out. I was coming out of Christ the King when one of the local church haunts approached me and asked in a menacing way, "Do you have a vocation?"

"No," I answered, "but how about yourself? I'm sure there are convents that will accept elderly women if they can bring a dowry." She looked at me, and her blue eyes turned to ice.

Pat Burns, a friend from Cincinnati and a fellow student at Catholic University, told me this story. One time before the Christmas holidays she was in a class taught by Monsignor Fulton J. Sheen. At the end of the class he gathered his books and left the room. But before the students could get up from their desks, he ducked back in and said, "Any of you who are afraid you have a vocation, you don't. Merry Christmas." Then he ducked back out again.

I should add that my friend from Xavier, who was so perceptive about what was bothering me, actually did have a vocation – as did his fiancée. Shortly after I talked with him, they decided to cancel their engagement and enter religious life.

As it turned out, I spent many hours lurking around the Department of Speech and

Drama, not a bad choice when I look back at it. The department head, Father Gilbert V. Hartke, had made CU's drama program one of the best in the country, a magnet for creative talent. He was already becoming nationally and internationally known. The drama students did wonderful musicals. One of the CU troupes had just toured the country, blowing everyone away with their youth, talent and energy.

One of the first plays I saw was *Oedipus Rex.* You know one of the things they say about tragedy is that it stuns you out of yourself. That's what happened. I still remember the final scene: Oedipus lying prone on the stage and the spotlight on his blood-covered hands.

Sometimes on the stage you can get too clever by half. That happened in a performance of *Macbeth.* When the witches appeared for the first time, they were dancing and chanting in front of Macbeth's castle. Then they ducked into the entrances of the castle towers and immediately appeared on the battlements, chanting the same lines. Well, of course, there were two sets of witches – not even witches can get to the top of a battlement that fast – but the audience missed several important lines of dialogue trying to figure out how they accomplished that feat.

Father Hartke allowed people who were not enrolled as drama students to be extras. In *The Mad Women of Chaillot*, I was one of the evil executives who go down the steps into the basement in search of her money and are obliterated. And during an evening of skits from George Bernard Shaw's plays, I had a brief moment in *Androcles and the Lion* – as the lion. I must have been pretty convincing because a little girl in the middle of the audience asked with some concern, "He's not a real lion is he?" I still do a low growl occasionally.

I also participated in a production of Yeats' *The Dreaming of the Bones,* based on Japanese Noh plays. Staged outside in the courtyard of the drama department, it was beautifully done in the quiet darkness of the arched walkway. I played a recorder and delivered from the shadows the sepulchral line: "Dry bones that dream are withered."

In the meantime, I had some excellent teachers. Professor J. Craig La Driere taught English Theory and Practice and had a great influence on me as a writer. Very early in my time at Catholic University, I witnessed a debate between La Driere and a distinguished Dante scholar. The debate turned on their differing approaches to Dante's *Divine Comedy.* La Driere was interested in the structure of the work. The Dante scholar was interested in Dante's platonic Christian viewpoint. It was basically a debate between an Aristotelian structural view of literature and a Platonic moral view.

That debate liberated me from trying to preach a sermon as a writer. To put it more simply: It freed me, even as I was writing from my Catholic faith, from the obligation of converting other people or myself. I don't know quite how to say this, but it let me see a piece of writing as a remarkably articulated object. That has stayed with me through many years of tinkering with poems. I always try to find the surprises that I could not have predicted.

Incidentally, when the poet Erza Pound was released from St. Elizabeth Hospital, he stayed with La Driere. Friends have told me that Pound would wake La Driere in the middle of the night wanting to fry up some eggs and talk. La Driere, I believe, went on to teach at Harvard and did not live but a few more years.

I continued writing at CU, though I certainly wasn't making any breakthroughs. I remember an over-wrought poem, I think it was verse drama, that one of the drama students blocked out for her master's thesis. I also attempted to write a script for a movie cartoon. My impulse to do this came from the fact that my cousin Alma was married to Conrad Radzinski, the creator of Mighty Mouse. They were doing quite well. The flatware in their house was gold instead of silver, and my Uncle Augie said they never ran anything on their TV except cartoons. But Conrad was a kindly man, and I admired him. I also got some advice from my friend Tom Gray, who had been a political cartoonist for the *Chicago Sun Times.*

As for the script, there were these monsters who were trying to take over the world. They were all defeated. At this point I don't know why. The hero was a duck. I am happy to say that no copies survive of this work.

I did better with my music. I purchased a beautiful banjo that I never learned to play – being left handed was an obstacle. But I did learn the saw, was passable on the recorder and quite good on the harmonica. The "Irish Washerwoman" and the introductory melody to Copeland's *El Salón México* were my show stoppers.

Luckily, I made some good friends at CU. I couldn't have survived without them. At the end of my first semester, some classmates asked me to join them in a basement apartment on a main avenue on the way to downtown Washington. I shared a room with Bob Browne, who still remembers the tag end of a poem I wrote: "*Despair has a bloody beak.*" It shows what shape I was in. There were four or five of us. Bob would spend his teaching career as professor of English at l'Universite de Montreal. Fred Crosson would marry Pat Burns and teach at Notre Dame; Paul Weiss would be one of the first people hired by the CIA (when I learned he had neglected to state on his application that he was teaching English at the Soviet Embassy, I told him to be sure to inform them of this); and Don Smith, who later became an editor of *U.S. News and World Report*.

After about a semester in the basement apartment, we moved to a house on Otis Street that was much closer to the university. It was just over the hill from a wooded city park that still had the defensive earthworks built during the Civil War.

The house had so much bedroom space that five or six people could live there at the same time, which meant we could always pay the rent. Al Emmons joined us and Ed Demers. Ed brought with him a whole library of folk music from around the world. I have two paintings of his. One is a bright spring scene with a man playing a banjo and a child listening. The other, "The Wabash Cannonball," is a night scene where one man plays the harmonica and another a guitar beneath a railroad trestle that a fast freight is about to cross.

We called the Otis Street house "The Chateau." Its backyard sloped into a woods of sorts and was covered with kudzu vines. When there was nothing better to do, we would attack the vines with hoes and rakes and anything else we had handy. The living room had a fire place, a wonderful amenity, especially on cold winter nights. We painted the interior and set up a volleyball court in the side yard. In the summers, we enjoyed a wide porch that spanned the front of the house. It was cool and pleasant to sit out there with friends.

Among them were girls who were doing their graduate work at Catholic University. Pat Burns, Annie MacMasters, and Ila Ware were three I remember. But there were others from the speech and drama apartment.

Another member of our Otis Street household was an old gray tomcat by the name of Ace. I always claimed that he could open beer bottles, but this may be an exaggeration. Ace added greatly to our sense of well-being:

> *he is a pretty good cat*
> *and if he is out playing*
> *with some other cats*
> *and you come down the sidewalk*
> *with two bags of*
> *groceries in your arms*
> *he won't pretend*
> *he does not know who you are*

In those days you could go around Washington and get these pick-up jobs. For a while I had a Saturday job reading newspapers for Press Intelligence. If, say, the Department of Agriculture was getting some bad press and wanted to know how extensive that was, they'd have you look for letters to the editor that were critical of the DOA. So whenever you'd pick up a letter like that, you would note it. If they were all the same, it meant that a very small group was parceling them around.

In a given month, Press Intelligence would have some forty accounts that they'd be checking into, and you would go through as many papers as you could and write a report on what you found. It was interesting because I got to read some excellent newspapers based in obscure places that I wouldn't have known about. Having read these papers, I know that their destruction by consolidation and takeover is a great loss to the country. And I became a marvelously fast reader. I remember surprising my friends when we visited Bull Run. I could read the bronze inscriptions at a glance.

Another memorable job was with the Bureau of Weights and Measures. The bureau was helping to create a new system of sizes for women's clothing. It was doing this at the request of the Mail Order Association, which wanted to get the sizes right so that there wouldn't be so many items returned. During the war, the Navy had had a problem with uniforms designed for the WAVES – they didn't fit. The Navy measured thousands of women, and eventually a system of standard sizes was devised, so that if a woman had a certain hip size, she could have a choice of three bust sizes. But now they wanted to change it to a choice of three hip sizes for each bust size – or something like that. The Bureau of Weights and Measures wanted somebody to tally the numbers and calculate the changes. The job had the title of statistician.

I shouldn't have been hired. However, the supervisor at the project had been a concert pianist who had been wiped out in the Depression and ended up working with the bureau, and the lawyer representing the Mail Order Association was a violinist who taught classics, I think, at Loyola. So they really didn't want a statistician to come in. They wanted somebody they could chat with, and I was the man.

I conscientiously added up columns of bust and hip measurements, consulted charts and wrote in the changes. I came in every morning and worked until noon until the project was completed. I have to admit, though, that all of this was done by hand with a pencil, and my sevens can be confused with nines. So if there are women today whose clothes don't quite fit, I am probably the one to blame.

Al Emmons, who was studying architecture, got me some work on a surveying team. I learned how to hold a plumb bob steady and to have a healthy respect for crews working highways in traffic where a stone kicked up by a tire can put out an eye. I also clerked at Bodkin Bookshop, but my most memorable job was at the annual Jackson Day dinner. President Truman was the keynote speaker, and college students were hired en masse to be waiters. I had no problem carrying the huge tray and placing the plates in front of the delegation from Maine. But when I served the coffee in a silver pitcher with a long, curved spout, I held it too high, and a stream of coffee shot out of the cup onto the starched shirt of a surprised and indignant congressman.

Meanwhile, the country was at war in Korea, and the Cold War was going on full force. After World War II, a number of the intelligence agencies had been dismantled. Now they were all being restored and reorganized, and the Naval Intelligence was trying to reconstitute its records. As a member of the Naval Reserves, I was involved in monthly meetings where people who had worked in the intelligence services spoke to us on various subjects. This is how I know that prior to World War II a woman highly placed in the Japanese Embassy would throw lavish parties in her Georgetown home for public officials and the Washington elite. As it turned out, she was telegraphing code to the Japanese government in the form of haikus.

I sometimes wonder what my life would have been like if I had been recruited by Naval Intelligence. All that became moot when I was reexamined again for my leg injury and declared "not fit for active duty." My naval career had finally ended.

My career at CU was ending too. I was passing the courses, but I felt washed out as a student. And my society there was beginning to break up. Friends were getting married and leaving for university posts around the country or for positions in the burgeoning FBI and the newly created CIA. Feeling more and more isolated, I packed up my banjo and drove home. I was thirty years old. I had credit hours but no degree and no job prospects. It was not a triumphant return.

John Knoepfle

Single in Cincinnati

I returned to my mother's two-family a-
partment on Pape Avenue in Hyde Park and to
the rooms I had renovated on the third floor. I
decided to see if I could earn a living writing for
magazines. I talked to other free-lance writers,
researched the market, queried editors and pub-
lished some articles. Over the course of the year,
I think I made about $350.

I supplemented that by taking on summer
work at Heekin Can Company. You would have a
long handled wooden fork with eight tines on it.
As the line of cans came down on the conveyor
belt, you would fork them up eight at a time and
set them into a box. Speed was important. The
conveyor belt never stopped, so you had to be
fast. The bigger cans were easier. You grabbed
them – three in each hand – and boxed them,
folded the box tops, taped them and stacked
them on a dolly. Sometimes you loaded the
boxes into big trucks. One afternoon coworkers
asked me what I was doing that evening.

"Going to see a Shakespeare play," I said.

"Who are you going with?"

"One of the Heekin girls."

In the community I grew up in, many of
the families I knew were people who had come
out of the Depression wealthy and were close to
the sources of their wealth. Because we had all
gone through the parochial school system, we
had an interlocking society where everyone knew
everyone else. In one year I dated thirty-eight
girls. Some of them broke my heart, and I broke
some hearts, too, I'm sorry to say. But I was also

a godsend for someone who didn't have a date on a weekend night, and she was a godsend for me. The brothers of some of the girls I dated tried to help me find employment. One friend got me a job as a trainee in a box corporation. To my despair and also to my great relief, I was let go. Among my classmates and fellow veterans, I was one of the few still at loose ends in the prosperous postwar boom.

But Cincinnati was a good place for me in other respects. The University of Cincinnati was bringing many poets in for their Elliston Lectures, which were free and open to the public. I met Stephen Spender, who wrote me a kindly letter, and Roy Campbell, among others.

In my solitariness I did a lot of reading. About this time I discovered the great Catholic novelists of France, the ones who wrote unflinchingly about the contemporary world and attacked the hypocrisy of the bourgeoisie.

A key author on this list was Leon Bloy. At the turn of the century he was the spiritual leader of a group of brilliant French writers and philosophers, including Raissa and Jacques Maritain. I was introduced to Bloy's work by *Pilgrim of the Absolute*, a collection of his journals, edited by Raissa. From there I moved on to the works of Georges Bernanos, Francois Mauriac and Charles Peguy.

I wasn't the only young writer reading these books. Heinrich Boll, the German novelist, was astonished by Bloy. Flannery O'Connor was influenced by him, as was J.F. Powers, author of *Morte D'Urban*. I was also reading Dostoyevsky, Tolstoy, Sigrid Undset and Graham Greene. And then there was Garcia Lorca. These writers were educating me far beyond my classroom experience and distancing me from the Catholicism of my boyhood. They were also giving me a whole new sense of what you could write about.

Meanwhile, my poems were being picked up and published around. A breakthrough came when the *Yale Review* printed "On a Fall Night." The first six lines reflect my bad banjo playing, far removed from the delicate picking in Appalachia. But I felt I was on my way as a poet.

> *Like some ungainly bird this banjo,*
> *Yet having a purpose on the wing,*
> *Here in the midmost Middle West*
> *I make a caterwaul of chords*
> *Undisciplined as Southern revivalists,*
> *Noisy as happily remembered minstrels.*

It wasn't long before Robert Lowell derailed my enthusiasm. I was taking his poetry workshop at the University of Cincinnati where he had the Elliston Chair. When I told him about my poem in the *Yale Review*, his reply was, "Well, they don't publish the best." I was devastated and stopped writing.

I Get a Job in Educational Television

Finally, in the fall of 1954, I got a job. Amazingly, it was because of the work I did at the Bureau of Weights and Measures. Joe Link, an old acquaintance from Xavier, was the public relations man for WCET – Cincinnati's new educational television station. It was scheduled to come on line in March of 1955. He asked me to tally and write up the results of a survey of potential viewers. Link was pleased with my work, and I was hired as the film editor for the fledgling station.

My job was to obtain films. We had no budget for rentals, so they had to be free. You got them anyway you could. You'd go to all the catalogs and write to people. They were promotional films, travelogues, documentaries. Some were embarrassingly promotional. For instance, I got a fairly good series on Native American cultures, except that in the films all the Indians were smoking Old Gold cigarettes.

My correspondence was extensive. I got a letter from the head of the musicians union, James C. Petrillo, and that awed our sound engineer. I wrote to the secretary of the Lebanese delegation to the United Nations asking for one of their promotional films. I noted in the letter how much I admired a famous philosopher who was the Lebanese ambassador to the U.N. I got a very cordial reply from the embassy and the film.

The TV studio was set up in a cavernous storage space in the attic of the Cincinnati Music Hall. To make the move to our new studio, we had to transfer boxes, desks and

66

filing cabinets from our current office. This was on the third floor of a nearby building that had steep, narrow stairs.

Remembering from the Navy the usefulness of lines, I purchased some coils of two-inch line and devised a way to lower all the furniture, boxes, and filing cabinets from our third floor office window. We snugged the line around the radiator footing, secured the boxes and cabinets with various squares and bowlines, and played the loads out over the window ledge. This attracted quite a few spectators. We had two students on the street holding guy lines to steady the loads, and two to receive them. Once we had everything on the ground, the students could cart it all up to our new offices via the elevator. It was a satisfying afternoon.

The wooden floor of our new studio had never been planed or sanded. As a result you couldn't make a smooth dolly with a camera. If you moved the camera around, the viewers got a tremor effect that sometimes went into earthquake. We also had problems with wiring. One night one of our two cameras caught on fire. I hastily went off the air with the other, the cameraman focusing for all he was worth on the WCET call letters painted on the side of the burning camera.

Bob Huber, the head of the station, was an experienced director. At WKRC Cincinnati, he had directed Rod Serling's *Twilight Zone* – and, indeed, Serling came to visit us early in the station's history. He told us he was always looking for nuances, quirks in his characters, things that set them apart and made them interesting, not stereotypical, human beings.

Huber took over the control room one evening and directed *Antigone*, as staged by a group of high school girls. He kept the lights down, chose his shots carefully to reveal the actors to the best effect and the chorus as it moved in circles left and right. It was an impressive evening. He maintained the scene in a half light so that there was a sense that the tragedy was taking place at the end of a darkening day. He showed us all what could be done with talent and experience.

Meantime, I had moved from being a film editor to director of the evening news. In those days, we had a sound man, plus three or four men on the controls, plus the floor men with the cameras and the boom mike. I was in the control room trying to keep track of everything. We took the news off the wire, and a professional newsman with a senatorial voice read it. I wrote brief commentaries to conclude the Friday evening newscast. He made them sound much better than they were.

It's hard to imagine this now, but I remember a period that lasted several days when you could open the newspaper and find no major conflicts reported anywhere. In response, I wrote a commentary about the world "poised in serenity." Of course, this was not really true. All kinds of things were going on that weren't being reported. I was sentimentalizing reality.

I don't remember women working the cameras at WCET, and none of the women on staff were directors. But some of the women students became directors, just as I had. Esther Pantagis and Dorothy Revelos were administrative staff. They set up and coordinated all the programs, especially the series. They had more television experience than I, as did the other director, John Morris.

The pay at WCET was not very good. I was making something in the neighborhood of subsistence. But I was happy to be where I was. The College of Music was next door, and I did my first teaching there – a class in Shakespeare. I can say now that Shakespeare probably survived it. When I left to go to South Bend, I gave the college my naval uniform for their opera performances. I imagine that it has made any number of appearances in *Madame Butterfly*. I also gave them my record of Howard Hansen's *Lament for Beowulf*, a powerful choral work with a challenge of trumpets at the end. And I have never heard it since.

It meant something to be in on the beginning of educational television. One afternoon at a program meeting, I pointed out that people driving along Columbia Parkway are looking down at the Ohio River mile after mile. I said, "We ought to do a series that would show what life is like if you're working on the river."

The response was, "Go out and do it."

Taping the River Men

I had no sense of how to begin, but I did have an RCA tape recorder. It was a big, unwieldy box that you had to plug in, but the voice pickup on those magnetic tapes was very fine. I began my project simply enough by obtaining the name of a river man who lived near me. He in turn gave me the names of others. I was also in touch with the U.S. Corps of Engineers and other people who worked on the river. We made maybe four or five shows.

On one program I interviewed some personnel from the Corps of Engineers about what they were doing and then we spliced in footage, which they provided, of the 1937 flood. I had played a part in that flood – I was about fourteen at the time and had worked as a volunteer, emptying trash cans full of debris down by the river. I remember the water had covered some of Eastern Avenue and was halfway up the side of the church of St. Rose of Lima.

When the Hiram College Showboat came to Cincinnati, I interviewed some of the students and they did a night of showboat vaudeville for us. The showboat had a calliope, a musical instrument fitted with steam whistles played from a keyboard. Sometimes the keys got so hot that the men had to wear gloves to play them. As it turned out, the one other boat on the river with a calliope happened to be docked at the Cincinnati landing at the same time we were doing the program. As a result, we had an historical night of dueling calliopes.

I also did a remote from the pilot house of the Omar, one of the last of the steam-driven stern-wheel coal tows actually working on the river. The pilot was Emory Edgington. By then boats like the Omar were a rarity. But before the age of diesel arrived in the 1940s, Emory and the other men I talked to were operating steam-driven stern-wheelers and side-wheelers on the inland waterways. The stern-wheel packets got their name because in the early days they carried the mail, but they also carried passengers, freight and livestock. The stern-wheel tows always pushed vessels before them, such as barges and showboats.

I remember when I taped Emory. It was in 1955, and he was in his nineties. He could remember his grandfather and his great grandfather. When you put those together, suddenly you are back to – not the first settlements in the valley certainly – but to the coming of the Europeans. That awed me.

Emory himself could look back to a boyhood in the 1870s. He knew the Ohio when it was filled with rafts made of walnut and oak logs five feet or more in diameter. They were being floated out on the river from forests in West Virginia and Kentucky to lumber yards in Cincinnati. He had started his career before the locks and dams were built, bringing wooden barges filled with coal down the Kanawha River during the spring raise.

All this appealed to my sense of history, but it was a kind of history that wasn't written down in books. Later, of course, what I was doing came to be known as oral history. Talking to these men changed my understanding of what history is and who should be included.

There was something whole about the work they did, the traveling here and there, the camaraderie that went with it. They had a society up and down the river that they were part of, and for them, to leave that society was to disappear. It had its own rules, its own ethics. For instance, the first three rows of corn along the river the shanty boaters could pick. If they picked in the fourth row, they would be shot.

Each man had his own style and rhythm of speaking. And what great story tellers they were! I was always careful to have them define the terms they used as it related to their work. For instance, they named the cabins on the packets after states. This is where the term "state room" comes from. The huge cabin on the upper deck was called "the Texas."

"Hogs" were the wires that ran up to the top of the boat from the bow and the stern. When you tightened them, "hogged it up," you stabilized the boat and made the deck slope so that rainwater would run off. If a stern-wheeler threw up a lot of spray, the river men called it a good "wet ass" boat.

Even after my tenure with the station had ended, I continued with the taping. I ended up speaking with over 50 men. Doing the tape recordings gave me a sense of place in the valley communities that I would never have had otherwise. It brought me in touch with a very admirable society of men. It gave me an ear for speech patterns that I wasn't finding in the literature I had been reading, and when I started writing about the river I tried to use that language. This work bent me towards a spoken rather than a written language.

At the same time I was reading Thomas Merton with great interest. I already knew *Seven Story Mountain*, but now I was reading poems he wrote at Gethsemane, the Trappist monastery downriver from Cincinnati in the hill country of Kentucky. These poems were suffused with the landscape Merton was living in. I realized that I could write from where I was and what I knew.

These are some lines from one of the first poems I wrote from that perspective.

Church of St. Rose of Lima, Cincinnati

It looks from the hill like something
Fra Angelico painted, the red
rectangular lines and the brick bell
steepled out of time. This church
honors St. Rose in a city
as spare of Peruvians as miracles.
It floods out whenever the river rises
and has a smell of common water
at the altars, and pilots of tows
on long hauls from Pennsylvania
needle the dark with searching lights
to catch the hour off her clock.

Football, Poetry and TV *at Notre Dame*

While we were still doing the river series, WCET ran out of money, and the programming – especially the kind I was doing – was eliminated. I was let go along with others, while the station waited for better days. Fortunately, a station was coming on line at Notre Dame University in South Bend, Indiana. Two of the directors came from WLW, a Cincinnati station. I had experience and was available. That got me the job of film editor for the station.

It turned out to be far removed from the work I was doing at WCET. Most of my job consisted of ordering and processing film. That meant looking at the whole movie, checking for blemishes and also – since this was Notre Dame – for possibly salacious scenes. I remember a movie about Russia – under the Czars, I believe – which had a wonderful climactic kiss at the end. We cut that off, leaving an enigmatic shot of crossed swords. But in this case, it wasn't because of the index of forbidden films but because of the Fighting Irish.

All our Saturday pre-game programs had to be "tailored," meaning "cut" when the team came on the field. But you never knew quite when that would happen. It was always touch and go on Saturdays when the team had a home game. One time I had to cut a western so that the last scene was the only thing that showed up on the screen. There was a cattle stampede under the title and a shootout, and then it was over. The viewers must have been puzzled.

One of the people who made the title slides couldn't spell, which proves that this problem is not recent. David "The General" Sarnoff, founder of NBC and head of RCA, came to the university to celebrate the new television station and to get an honorary degree. The speech he made on that occasion would be quoted several years later by Marshall McLuhan in *Understanding Media.* Sarnoff said: "We are too prone to make technological instruments the scapegoats for the sins of those who wield them." It was all too true. When the slide announcing the celebration came up on the screen, it read: "General Smearoff receives onery degree." I was enjoying an evening with Fred and Pat Crosson when this came on the screen. Pat had worked for WLW. We had a good laugh.

I would often go with Fred to have lunch with the younger Notre Dame faculty. When he mentioned that I was a poet, I told them that I had stopped writing because Robert Lowell had dismissed my work. This word got to another young poet, John Logan, who was teaching the Great Books at the university. Logan was at a very fine moment in his career. He had just published *Cycle for Mother Cabrini*, and it was getting good reviews. In fact, Ezra Pound had written him a cordial letter about it, which Logan's children had marked up with crayons. Logan looked up my poem in the *Yale Review.* He told me that he couldn't understand what had possessed Lowell to trash the poem. He said it was an interesting poem with a lot of verbal excitement. His verdict was: "You don't need a teacher. You need an editor." I owe a great deal to those words. With Logan's encouragement I began writing again.

The scene at South Bend was good. I had friends I could talk to. Besides Fred and Pat and John and his wife Gwen, my old friend Jack Hoenemeyer and his wife Marsha lived in nearby Elkhart where Jack worked as a salesman. Through Logan I got to know John Carroll and other Chicago writers. I remember attending in a packed auditorium a wonderful reading by e. e. cummings. Besides reading his own poems, he added poems by other writers and anonymous border ballads and told us why he liked them.

A new friend was Bob Christin, a young Notre Dame English instructor. He became very important in Upward Bound, a program funded during the War on Poverty by the U.S. Office of Economic Opportunity. School counselors recommended students who weren't achieving but who had promise, and Upward Bound gave them a summer of intensive study on a college campus. To the university's credit, the program Christin founded at Notre Dame is still in operation in the same spirit as the original. This holds true for a number of colleges and universities that have kept the program alive on their campuses.

I write about this because in the 1960's, I was a consultant for Upward Bound and visited projects on Indian reservations in South Dakota and Wisconsin, low-income communities in Mississippi, Tennessee, Kentucky, Arkansas, and the South Side of Chicago. This meant a great deal to me. It wasn't just the getting around to places I would never have known. It was meeting so many dedicated people and seeing the students respond to these new opportunities. It was a privilege to be part of that.

In a poem called *A Gathering of Voices,* I quote one of the counselors at the Spearfish Canyon Upward Bound Project.

> *near the rosebud the santee said*
> *its when its dark the fears slip out*
> *I wont leave this dorm*
> *when there is one child restless*

When Upward Bound was terminated by the Nixon administration, I received a shabby mimeographed dismissal letter. But I still cherish the print with a quote from Tolstoy that the Washington office of Upward Bound sent its consultants: "I sit on a man's back, choking him and making him carry me, and yet assure myself and others that I am very, very sorry for him and wish to lighten his load by all possible means – except by getting off his back."

To get back to the Notre Dame station – it was a blend in which the commercial end was supposed to support the educational. In other words, the salespeople received the bonuses, and the production staff the belt tightenings. WLW was held up to me as a model, but I had friends at WLW and one time when I was home I visited there. I was astounded at the easy opulence of the place and amazed to learn that the WLW film editor had more than one projector and did not have to preview and repackage every film that came into the station. I decided I had had enough of this.

My brother Neal, who was now a prosperous car salesman, would fix me up with impressive cars that often turned out to be junkers. The one I had at South Bend ran all right, but in the winter snow entering through some leak in the hood would cover my shoes. With my severance pay from the Notre Dame station, I bought a turquoise and white four-door Chevy sedan. It was a classic beauty, the last model before those exaggerated fins were added that wrecked a whole series of 1950's cars.

I was not worried. Besides my new car, I had a contact for a new job. Ohio State University was bringing an educational station on line in the spring of 1956. They said they wanted me on the staff and would write me a letter formalizing the offer.

John Knoepfle

Not Broke but Unemployed

Back in Cincinnati by Christmas, I busied myself working on a manuscript, sending poems out for publication and writing the occasional free-lance article. I remember visiting John Bunker, the father of one of my classmates, to talk about spending a lifetime being a poet. Bunker, who had published books of his own, was part of Stephen Vincent Benet's circle and had been Joyce Kilmer's secretary. He told me that publishing a book of poems is like dropping a rose petal into the Grand Canyon and waiting to hear it hit bottom. I can witness to the accuracy of his statement.

I was also corresponding with Logan in South Bend, rich in the knowledge that I had a friend and ally. When someone wrote me a snide letter about the "Church of St. Rose of Lima," Logan shot back that he was a literary snob, not interested in poems about the Midwest. I applied for the University of Cincinnati's annual Elliston Chair poetry workshop and was accepted.

With time on my hands and in search of subjects for articles, I began dropping in on Edward Doering, a lawyer and a professor of English at Xavier University. I had heard that he had been involved in the defense of the Japanese accused of war crimes in the postwar trials in Japan. As I look back on our conversations, I realize that he was quietly telling me things that were at variance with the official viewpoint of World War II. It was generally accepted that atrocities occurred in all the Japanese prison camps. Doering said that this depended on the integrity of the commander of the camp. If the commander prohibited the abuse of prisoners, there were no atrocities. The responsibility, Doering said, was on the commanders.

He also told me that because of the need for skilled manpower during the Occupation, a man who might have headed a crew of dock-workers in the United States would be commissioned as a Major. Many of those men had no idea how to wield the unlimited power they were given and committed unspeakable atrocities against the Japanese. He told me that his report on the Occupation and the abuses that he had noted was buried somewhere in the Washington bureaucracy.

I also took classes from Herbert Schwartz, a charismatic philosopher who had doctorates in mathematics and music and was a convert to Catholicism. He had come to Xavier from Notre Dame, and I was part of a group of people who were interested in what he had to say about living the faith. Howard Hart, a Cincinnati poet and contemporary of mine, also turned up at the Schwartz house. He had recently returned from the Left Bank where he had been translating contemporary French poets and philosophers and writing poems of his own.

Hart had worlds to say about thinkers and philosophers whom I didn't know anything about, and I would counter by inventing thinkers and philosophers to controvert whatever he was saying. Over the years I have regretted this and have felt the loss of his friendship rather keenly.

Bill Madden, an old friend from Xavier High School, was now earning his Ph.D. in

Victorian studies. While he finished his doctorate, he and his wife Carol were living in the attic apartment of a mansion they were caretaking. I visited them often. Madden shared my interest in Leon Bloy and the French Catholic modernists. He would go on to a long career teaching at the University of Indiana in Bloomington and heading the English Department at the University of Minnesota in Minneapolis.

At this time I also became acquainted with a group of Catholic families living in Newtown, just outside of Cincinnati. Part of a back-to-the-land movement, they had built a school on the foundations of a barn set in the side of a hill. Heated by a wood stove, it had stone walls on three sides and wall-to-ceiling glass windows on the fourth. They had hired a young man named Robert Spencer to teach their children. I was fascinated by Spencer's teaching ability and got to know him and his wife Edith. He would go on to Vermont where he would be elected to the state Senate, and we would meet again 17 years later. He was the founding president of an innovative school in Springfield, Illinois, called Sangamon State University, and I would be hired there in 1972, the third year of the school's operation.

I was also a friend of Ray Pater, who had served in the Army in Europe. We often went to visit his uncle, an Aquinas scholar of some ability, who was happy to read passages from the works of St. Thomas and explain them to us.

Ray Hellman, my closest and oldest friend from Xavier High School, had earned his M.D. and married Rita Lutmer, the sister of another high school friend. They were starting their family – five children: four sons who became doctors and a daughter who is currently a candidate for the Ohio 12th District Appellate Court. Tom Clarke had gotten married and was beginning a lifelong career with the FBI Tom Grey, another old friend, had married Clarke's sister, Connie. I often visited with Gray when I was recuperating from my operation at the Great Lakes Naval Hospital. He did a cartoon of me with an admiral's hat on, assaulting a beach despite the loss of my head, and one afternoon did an oil sketch of me, which I still have. He had settled down in Cincinnati and with another friend, Julian Kokenge, had founded a commercial art business. So, except for being a bit lonely and too much in demand as a best man, I was on good terms with my life.

Then one winter day I chanced to meet John Morris, my old friend from WCET. He asked me, "Why didn't you get in touch with Ohio State?" He told me they had written me a letter formally offering me a position as a program director, and when I did not reply, they had hired someone else. Stunned, I told John I had never received the letter. It must have gotten lost in the mail. Once again, I was without work and without prospects for work.

John Knoepfle

I Meet Peggy at a Poetry Workshop

Once again, old friends from high school and college tried their best to keep me employed. I shingled roofs of new houses. I did the cleanup job before these houses were exhibited for sale. I put in a concrete base for an air conditioner, and I helped redo the wiring for an elegant cocktail lounge near Fountain Square. When we took the marbled panels off the walls, we found vermin swarming behind them. That memory turned up in *Prayer Against Famine.*

heroin

look now in the elegant cocktail lounge
look at these glass topped tables
and the vermin at the edge of the wall
swarming beneath the carpet

where the demon of kells
ragged and starving into his bones
presses his nose up under those tables
and splits his face with a grin

Desperate for permanent work, I took some multiple choice tests for a position with Blue Cross, a big Cincinnati employer. I remember one of the questions: "Would you rather climb a mountain, become a corporate executive, or read to blind children?" Of course, I put down "climb a mountain," although I thought it would have been safer to "become a corporate executive." But if the question had been asked "Which of the three you have done?" I would

83

have put down the obvious, "Read to blind children." I did not get the job, although the man who had administered the test said he wanted to talk to me further.

I also applied without success for a position as an ad man for Bell Telephone. Evidently my metaphors were too Shakespearean. One of them had to do with being crowned a king with the purchase of a Bell phone.

The Elliston poet that year was Peter Viereck. He was a short and rather slight man with graying auburn hair and a beard. He had won the 1949 Pulitzer Prize for a book of poems entitled *Power and Decorum,* and his book *Conservatism Revisited: the Revolt Against Ideology* had made him a spokesman for postwar conservatives. This created a silent classroom. Most of the students were either not interested in politics or far to the left of Viereck.

He was interested in traditional rhymes and meters, which was not where I was as a poet. However, I did a sonnet for him entitled "*Sparrows.*" It reflected both my debt to Robert Lowell and Gerard Manley Hopkins and my unhappiness with my current situation.

Why is it pain holds us something less
Than fodder for the barns of death, and slain
Across your years, not with joy you bless
Our lot, but beat us down like storm shot grain?
Lord, these proletarian birds are worth
A world for haven: where is our ransomed earth!

That Easter I was able to get a date with Peggy Sower, a junior at the University of Cincinnati, who was also attending the workshop. And from there we had a memorable summer. I was intrigued by the fact that she had recently come back from Peru, South America, where she had been a student at San Marcos University, perhaps the oldest university in the Americas. She could talk about Dostoyevsky and other authors I was interested in, but she could also recite the names of the fourteen Inca kings.

And she had a family. Her father, an engineer, was working on an irrigation project in Bolivia. Until her teenage years Peggy had lived in Colorado and then at Anderson Ranch Dam on the South Fork of the Boise, the tallest earth dam in the world at the time. The family had been in Peru because her father was working on an irrigation project there. Now her mother was in Cincinnati with three daughters – Peggy; Elinor, a Freshman at the University of Cincinnati, and Molly in high school at St. Mary's. Her brother Jim was at the University of Colorado. Rudolf Ludeke and Carlos Delgado were two friends of Jim's from Peru. They were now living with Peg's mother and sisters and attending the University of Cincinnati also. Spending time with that family was a new experience for me, the youngest of four brothers. I admired Peggy's mother and her exotic brood, and they made me feel at home there.

Peggy, who had studied the pre-Colombian civilizations of Peru, was fascinated to learn that people were living in Ohio more than 2000 years ago. The Great Serpent Mound, built by the

Adena people – and located in Adams County, of course – had not yet become a pilgrimage site for those seeking sacred places. The two of us – we were the only ones there that morning – could stretch out with our heads propped on the flank of the good serpent, entertained by an excitement of indigo buntings and yellow warblers.

On another trip, we climbed Fort Hill – appropriately located in Hillsboro – a hilltop enclosure built by the Hopewell people. We went up a trail tangled with brambles that looked like it hadn't been used since the enclosure was built 2000 years before. We visited Fort Ancient, another Hopewell site, a ceremonial gathering place, overlooking the Little Miami River, one of the most beautiful places in Ohio.

We didn't know then that the Great Serpent Mound was aligned with the winter and summer solstice points, or that Fort Ancient was an astronomical clock with mounds marking the solstices and gaps marking the lunar year. But we sensed the enormous power of these places, far beyond what we could see and understand.

We visited the big circle mounds and geometric shapes at the Mound City group in Chillicothe on the Sciota River. And we wandered the Madisonville site there at Mariemont, which for some reason that I do not understand is now beneath a subdivision of expensive houses.

The Shakespeare plays at Yellow Springs. were another favorite destination. We picnicked at Antioch College one summer afternoon before the play began. Peggy had baked a loaf of bread for the occasion. I was impressed. She still does

– bake bread and impress me – and has for fifty-one years.

And one summer evening in a bar in Mount Lookout she bought me a beer with some of the prize money she had received for two essays about her life in Peru. My friends treated me with scorn and contempt because I had let a girl buy me a beer. Tom could not believe I had accepted a handout from a date. It was a breech of decorum.

In the meantime, I had picked up a summer job with Hans Wachtel, a landscape architect. I think he hired me because he wanted someone to talk to. We became good friends, and I spent a number of cheerful evenings with him and his wife discussing literature. My job with Wachtel was to work with the rest of his crew on whatever landscaping job came up. We weeded, cut brush, planted, and sprayed lawns for people who wanted to have garden parties free of chiggers and mosquitoes. The foreman and I were white. The others in the crew were black. They accepted me. We worked hard, and I learned a lot from them.

On her way down Dana Avenue to classes at the University of Cincinnati, Peggy often saw me coming in the opposite direction in the back of a swaying truck bristling with chemicals and garden tools. I was in route with the crew to a day's work at some Cincinnati estate. I didn't realize it at the time, but my failure to get a corporate job and join the mainstream meant something to her. She was still in culture shock from her time in Peru. She had seen poverty and oppression there. There were bullet holes in the walls of San Marcos University from tanks sent in by President Manual Odria, the current U.S.-supported dictator. Peggy was ill at ease with her country. It seemed to her that I, too, did not fit in and that she had at last found someone who could be a companion.

The books I was reading were also, she told me later, a lifeline for her. She had never heard of Mauriac or Greene. She loved these books because the heroes and heroines had failed on many fronts and committed huge numbers of sins and yet still lived in a world that was holy. She listened to me talking to other people about St. Thomas Aquinas, took what she needed and ignored the rest. Without knowing it, I gave her back her faith.

At the end of May, Peggy was in the throes of final exams and about to get an incomplete on a term paper. To save her from further distress, I dictated to her a paper on "Hamlet as Student." Later we went out to Fritsch's for fish and tartar sauce sandwiches and chocolate milkshakes, my accustomed treat for dates in my reduced financial circumstances. As it turned out, the paper got a C, but at least Peggy was not stuck with anymore papers.

Instead, under the impression that we were not suited for each other, she got on a Greyhound bus and went to California to visit her Aunt Elinor in Escondido. I was not aware that she had left town and did not find out until a week or two later when I met Carlos at the Shell Station on Erie Avenue and asked him how she was doing.

While I was mulling this over, Peggy relented, and a box soon came in the parcel post containing jars of jam made from plums growing in her aunt's back yard, the lids decorated with pink paint and small shells. This pretty well determined our fate.

Remembering Peter Viereck's poetry workshop after all these years, I have to say that everyone in it had talent and I suspect that all of them, like Peggy, continued writing. But the only one I know of besides myself who made a career writing is Alvin Green-berg. He is still writing poems, short stories, novels and librettos for operas. He has won many prizes, including the Ohiana prize and most recently the Idaho Prize. He has long been a friend and presently lives in Boise with his wife, the poet Janet Holmes.

Years later, Peggy and I read a tribute to Peter Viereck in the New Yorker. *We learned that in his long career as a teacher and writer, he had maintained his integrity. Critical of liberals, he had also denounced the neoconservatives, whom he found far removed from his vision of a new conservatism. And so we understood a little better the character of the man whose poetry workshop brought us together.*

Comp and Circumstances

I continued to work with Wachtel's crew for the rest of the summer. Dogs liked us. One day when we were eating lunch in the backyard of a big estate, the house cocker spaniel came down to see if he could get a handout. One of the men threw the dog a piece of sandwich, saying "Yeah, and he eats pork chops for breakfast." In another yard, where the foreman was directing us setting bricks for a patio, two big German shepherds ran off with the bricks.

But as the summer wore on, I began to understand that the men I worked with didn't have the options that I had. I remember sitting in the truck with George, who wanted to know if "that building across the street" was a hospital.

I said, "No, George, that is Xavier University."

He thought a while. Then he said, "Did you go to high school, John?"

I said, "I was here at this university for a number of years."

He said, "Well, if you was here, what in the hell is you doing pulling up weeds with me for?"

I said, "You know, I can't answer that."

I knew then that there had to be something I could do that wouldn't be taking someone else's job pulling weeds. By then it was late summer. I wrote to Ohio State to see if I could pick up a job teaching English. I got an answer by return mail. They were shorthanded, I guess, and the fall semester was only weeks away.

John Knoepfle

In September 1956, I arrived at Ohio State University and joined a roomful of young instructors teaching Freshman Composition, if I remember right. About thirty of us were assigned to one room called "The Bullpen" in spite of the fact that many of these young instructors were women. We each had a battered wooden desk and a wooden swivel chair, and that was pretty much the sum total of our office equipment. My salary was $3,600 a year, which we figured amounted to about twenty-five cents a theme. Nevertheless, it felt good to be there. I was thirty-three years old. I had found a job that might take me somewhere. I was among my peers and, indeed, I have to say that many of them were my betters.

A good friend was Sam Schaeffer. He had finished his course work for a doctorate at the University of Chicago. A fine poet, he was fascinated by the work of Wallace Stevens. And there was Perry Gianakos, who I believe had completed his work in American Studies from Duke University. Sam was good to Perry and me. He helped us firm our sometimes sketchy knowledge of our teaching assignments. He made sure that Perry and I understood such things as the nature of the compound-complex sentence and the proper use of the semi-colon. Once I caught on, I became a tyrant in the matter of the disposition of semi-colons.

I remember full moon nights over the Olentangey River and handsome artifacts of stone, mica, clay and flint at the state museum. An old Xavier friend from Cincinnati, Jack Wilson, was doing research in Columbus. He was an M.D., married and a father by then. We enjoyed going out for a couple of beers. My life was secure now, but it only deepened a feeling of emptiness. I was despondent with being single. When I came back to Cincinnati to visit Peggy, she remembers being surprised – given the shakiness of our relationship – that my main subject of conversation was the roominess of my basement apartment.

In December I decided to ask Peggy to marry me. It was evening, already dark. I walked to the drugstore on the corner near my apartment complex and called Peggy on the pay phone there. I proposed, and she accepted. We agreed that if we decided to wait for a June wedding, we would probably break up. Not wanting that to happen, we set the date for December 26, a little over two weeks away.

With my vast experience as a best man, I had already calculated the time it would take to read the publication of the banns to matrimony. They had to be read on three successive Sundays (in case anyone had an objection to the marriage). By then there were only two Sundays left before Christmas, but Christmas was a Holy Day and counted as a bann day, also.

It was audacious. I got away with it because of the naiveté of Peggy and her mother Agnes on the subject of weddings. Peggy had never given much thought to marriage, and her parents had been married during the Depression in the rectory of the Cathedral in Denver, Colorado – each arriving on a different train.

Peggy's mother was as naïve about the protocol of Cincinnati parishes as she was about weddings. The Sower home was in St. Cecilia Parish, but Agnes preferred to attend Mass at St. Mark's. Her mistake was confiding this to the pastor of St. Cecilia's. He replied that her daughter had better go to St. Marks to get married. Agnes went to St. Marks and again was overly truthful. The pastor's response was that Agnes had no legal standing as a parishioner and her daughter could not be married in his church.

It doesn't matter, I told them. "I will go to Xavier University and see if we can get married in Bellarmine Chapel." But as it turned out, this too was prohibited because of the lateness of the date and the Christmas holidays coming on. For a moment I thought we could go across the river to Kentucky and commandeer a justice of the peace. Happily, I had one option left. My brother Rudy was a favorite son of Christ the King Parish in Mount Lookout and its pastor, Monsignor Quinn. Rudy was granted permission to perform our marriage at Christ the King.

Peggy's brother Jim came home for the holidays with his leg in a cast, ending his career on the Colorado Buffaloes football team. Her father arrived from Bolivia just in time to receive a telegram from the archdiocese of Denver stating that Peggy had been baptized and confirmed. I still remember how the expression on his face changed as he read the last item. It stated that his daughter had married a man named F. Baur Betz in the spring of 1954.

Once it was determined that this was a clerical error, Peggy's father and her Aunt Elinor took out their false teeth, poured themselves a couple of bourbons and had a wonderful time reminiscing. My own mother was so happy that I was at last getting married that she gave me a beautiful diamond ring that had belonged to my Aunt Madeleine for the engagement ring. Sam took me to various Columbus stores and saw to it that I had a proper blue suit for the wedding, rather than the broad shouldered gangster out-fits the salesmen were trying to sell me.

Because a new church was being con-structed, we were married in the school gym-nasium. It was beautifully decked out with pine boughs and poinsettias. Tom Crain stood best man, and Peggy's sister, Elinor, was the brides-maid. I remember when we stepped into the cold air of that winter morning, I saw the snowflakes caught in Peggy's dark hair.

What to say about that winter and spring. The couple in the apartment above us com-plained that they were being overheated. And Peggy got pregnant almost immediately. We did not obey the advice of one of the deans, who told me, "Let your wife live with her mother for a cou-ple of years and concentrate on your doctorate."

In a photo Peggy's father took of us as we left for Columbus, I am wrapped in a volum-inous overcoat, and she is carrying a little blue overnight case very much like the one Jane Fonda carries in *Period of Adjustment*. Watching that movie is part of our Christmas festivities.

> *love is like a bowl*
> *so when you break it*
> *glue it together*
> *if it won't hold water*
> *fill it with apples*

94

John Knoepfle

Becoming a Father and Finding a Job

That winter, my project of taping the river
men was written up in both of the Columbus pa-
pers. This helped me find more old timers to talk
to. Peggy accompanied me on many of these
interviews. We met Captain Savage, who at the
turn of the century had journeyed up the Ama-
zon on a steamboat, and Curtis Marshall, who
had lived on the river as a young boy in Gal-
lipolis. He sat in an easy chair telling us stories
and flicking his cigar ashes on the plush carpet.
A huge parrot sat on a perch next to him, lis-
tening to it all.

At the end of the school year at Ohio
State, I spread out a map of the United States,
and with Peggy watching in fascination set a
compass so that the circle I drew would fall
within the confines of the upper Mississippi
watershed. That's where I felt I should be in
order to continue my recordings. I got a reply
from the University of West Virginia in Morgan-
town and from Southern Illinois University in
Carbondale. SIU was opening two residence
centers, one in East St. Louis and one in Alton.
The latter, the head of the English Department
in Carbondale wrote, would be ideal for me
because there was a lock and dam there and
many river men. I chose the Alton residence
center – the salary was a princely $4,100 a year;
Morgantown offered only $3,800.

Since I had no job over the summer, we
took over the vacant first floor apartment of my
mother's house on Pape Avenue and got by on
my disability payment. Mom was delighted to

have her pregnant daughter-in-law living in her house. The new baby would be a cousin to Bill and Edie's ten-year old son Stephen. Mom liked Peggy and regaled her with stories. Edith complained with some justification that my mother hadn't had time yet to zero in on Peggy. But Mom may have known better than any of us that she had little time left. That summer she complained of backaches, and in the fall she would learn that the cancer she had received surgery for a few years earlier had returned.

But those days were long and pleasant. My brother Rudy came home to visit. Neal had the back bedroom in my mother's apartment upstairs. Peggy's father had taken on an engineering project in Burma, but her mother and the rest of the family were still in the house on Grovedale near Withrow High School. Sowers and Knoepfles and Cincinnati friends made for a pleasant society.

If the baby was a boy, we would name him John Simeon – after myself and a prophet in the New Testament. Several of my friends also named their sons after obscure prophets, and many of these names were changed when their sons got old enough to defend themselves. John Simeon became John Michael. The name we picked for a girl was Catherine Lorena – the Catherine after my mother and Lorena, the name of a steamboat which was named after a civil war song.

In midsummer, I received a letter informing me that I had been relocated to East St. Louis and should report to the residence center there in mid-September. Because the baby was

96

not due until the end of September, we planned that Peggy would move back to her mother's house, while I went on to Illinois to find a place for us to live. But young John arrived before I left – on Labor Day, of course, September 3, 1957. We had gone to Cowan Lake State Park for a picnic with Peggy's mother, Elinor and Molly. After we came back in the early afternoon, Peggy's water broke. When she called her mother to ask what this meant, the reply was, "Get to the hospital!"

John was born at Good Samaritan. In the dim light, I saw him carried out in the arms of a nurse just ahead of the gurney carrying Peggy. He was long and lean and flecked with blood, and he weighed six pounds, three ounces. Peggy, looking up from the gurney, groggily remarked, "I love you." I was pleased, although I knew she had been drugged or something.

A week later, I went west, driving along the Ohio river bluffs and bottom lands as much as possible. I interviewed river men here and there along the way. Then I traveled across southern Illinois to speak with the head of the English Department at SIU Carbondale and on then by sundown north into Belleville and a motel room.

That night I thought I would take a look at East St. Louis and drove into the town through the intense heat of late summer. The street-lamps were swarming with big green gnats. I turned here and there, leaving the main street behind and soon was lost in utter darkness. And so I parked. I would know later that I was in the flats near the bridges between the city and the levee. I sat there in the car, perplexed and, yes, afraid, not knowing what would happen next.

Then from a pile of buildings to my left – I could just make out the shapes in the darkness – there came the clear notes of a trumpet, a sound like a baptism in that torrid night. I would learn later from those I told this story to that I was hearing Miles Davis, returned from New York to visit his old neighborhood. So I listened, and then after a time I turned the key in the ignition and drove back to the main part of town without an error and on to my motel room. That was my introduction to East St. Louis, a place of poverty and trouble and genius and hope. I would be there for the next four years.

John Knoepfle

East St. Louis

When I reported to the residence center
the next morning, I discovered that I was the
only full-time employee in the English Depart-
ment, which consisted of myself and three part-
time instructors. None of us had Ph.D.'s. At first
we were housed along with some kindergarten-
ers in a new primary school building. I remem-
ber we had to crawl on our knees to write on the
blackboard. And an elderly math instructor told
me that when he sat on the john, he felt like a
grasshopper. Then we moved to the old Horace
Mann High School at 10th and Ohio – we had
half of the building.

In contrast, the Alton Residence Center
was housed in Shurtleff College, a Baptist sem-
inary that had recently closed. It was a campus
of fine old buildings, stately trees, and benches
with inscriptions, such as, "Carpe diem – Class
of 1894." The Alton center was staffed with pro-
fessors, not instructors, and they all had their
Ph.D.'s. Does that tell you something?

Our East St. Louis students came from a
variety of backgrounds. As I remember, some
thirty percent were second generation from the
delta regions of the South. Others were sons and
daughters of Italian miners or of Ukrainians and
Lithuanians who worked in the steel mills at
Granite City. There were students from towns
along the Mississippi who could trace their
lineage back to the French settlers and even
earlier – and students of German descent whose
great-grandfathers built those brick cottages in

Belleville. There were Turkish students and the sons and daughters of gypsies also.

For the most part, they were glad to have the opportunity to enroll in the new classes. Some thought my "Yes, mother, I have three" sentence traced through many Indo-European languages was very interesting. It was not my own. However, I have forgotten the source. And my comp theme structured on the careful study of both sides of a Lincoln penny held some interest as well. There were moments that I cherish. Once I asked a class, "Who would you rather have control over the atom bomb – Khrushchev or your minister?" And they all yelled, "Khrushchev!"

I learned early not to assign emotionally charged topics. Even a title like "My Ideal Bedroom" had its problems. For students sharing a room with five or more siblings, a dream of a private space would outrun laws of grammar. One of my themes, quite popular, was "How to Wrap a Christmas Present." You could not compose this theme out of simple enthusiasm. It was a challenging exercise. One part was to be written in simple sentences, one in complex sentences, one in compound and one in compound-complex. There was even a small section that could be done in fragments and one using semicolons. This assignment may have reflected my own exhilaration when I mastered these things under the tutelage of Sam Schaffer. There was one other caveat. The students could not assume that their readers had any idea of what a pair of scissors was, for instance.

John Knoepfle

In my second year of teaching, I enrolled at St. Louis University as a graduate student in English. Reading heavily in the literature of the English Renaissance, I learned that Erasmus, the great teacher and humanist, had come to England at the behest of John Fisher, Bishop of Rochester. Many of the formulas that distinguish English Renaissance writing date from this time and were introduced by Erasmus. For instance, his formula for "How to write about a country" was adopted by English sea captains, to describe their explorations and discoveries. I also learned the formula for praising a person and shared this knowledge with my students.

If you want to write about a person, then you describe the country he comes from, the town of his birth, his ancestors, his distinguished parents, his education, events in his life, and the accomplishments that make him worthy of praise. Then you conclude with a "clarkly" comparison. I used this with good results everywhere I taught – at the residence center, at St. Louis University High School, at the Mark Twain Summer Institute in St. Louis and in freshman classes at Maryville College, as well as in various workshops for teachers. Students always did well with this formula, and I know that it has been used on at least one occasion for a eulogy.

At St. Louis University, I read John Fisher's *Exposition of the Seven Penitential Psalms* and found unexpected correspondences. Writers in Tudor England were using a language that was similar to the language of most of my students. It was an English written before the

101

printers standardized the spelling and the grammarians attached a Latin-based grammar to the language. Curiously, it reminded me of the papers that my students were writing. Their so-called errors were almost identical to the uncapitalized, unpunctuated texts with multiple spellings of the same word that John Fisher and his peers wrote.

The difference was that the Tudor preachers were highly educated in Latin, so there were tropes and flourishes that did not appear in my students' themes – though the students had their own rhetoric and it could be quite powerful. I had to read their work out loud with an ear cocked to the sound of the voice. Otherwise I would miss both the meaning and the power of their sentences.

I cannot say that I succeeded any better as a teacher, but I did gain more understanding and was perhaps less judgmental about my marginal students. I can remember, midway through the quarter, letting my classes know that many students were probably not going to pass the course. But since it would take the school registrar two years to catch up, I advised them to keep on taking courses. They might be able to claim two years of college, which would help when they were job hunting. And if they passed their other courses, why then they could take the comp class again when they were seniors and perhaps pass it. Some of them did this. Years later, to my surprise, my saucy daughter Molly at SIU Carbondale did the very same thing with her Freshman math requirement – passed it in her senior year.

In East St. Louis, it was hard to get to the river. The one time I saw the Mississippi close up from the river side of the East St. Louis levee, it was winter. The river was jammed with ice, and I had a sense of it as an ominous presence.

Coal sells a bushel a week
at MacArthur Bridge.
Time weighs men by the peck
in the shacks there,
and the January dark
denies a summer delta.
Ice grinds the winter
river, a savage business.

I did manage to tape record several Missouri pilots – and discovered that the Missouri is a much different river from the Ohio. If your boat ran aground, you waited until the river shifted and washed away the sandbar under the keel. You had to have patience. I tape recorded Captain Menke on his showboat at the St. Louis landing and was able to tell him that I had seen his father's citizenship papers in an antique store in Cincinnati. Though I did record a few interviews later on, my career as a collector of oral histories had ended. The tapes are presently housed in the Public Library of Cincinnati and Hamilton County and also, with transcripts, at the Oral History Collection at the University of Illinois Springfield.

Much of my first book, *Rivers into Islands*, is filled with what I learned from the river men and from my students at the East St. Louis Residence Center. My sense of the East Side so heavily industrialized, so full of ostentatious wealth and deep poverty – I tried to catch that in "Night Fire." The oil refinery is the Wood River refinery on the floodplain between East St. Louis and Alton.

> *Above the oil refinery*
> *the torch howls in the wind,*
> *flaring and contracting*
> *among the millionaires.*
> *It snaps there.*
> *Smoke trails underneath it,*
> *and I think it resembles*
> *a severed head on a platter,*
> *a John Baptist lurid in sparkles*
> *of Bedouin hand bells.*
> *I drive down the road,*
> *then it leaps up again,*
> *grinning in the car mirror*
> *like a colored porter in a plush hotel,*
> *or a flame that roars in its solitude.*

The East Side was rich in history and folklore, a complex place. I encouraged my classes to collect oral histories and local folklore. For instance, that fertile floodplain, the American Bottoms, was the biggest producer of horseradishes in the United States. My students told me about longstanding feuds between owners of different horseradish patches, which flared into wars during the Depression. I learned that steelworkers in Granite City passed the time during their midnight break by tossing chunks of slag at the rats.

John Knoepfle

A student whose uncle had been a hobo in the 1930s told me about the signs hobos chalked on fences and buildings to communicate with one another. I've forgotten them all except one – a picture of a plump pussy cat. It means that the woman of the house is kind and will feed you a good meal. I learned about the 1918 flu epidemic hitting the river towns and the things people did to cope with it. In response to this wealth of material, I began writing story poems and poems with many voices. "Country Sweat" is about the flu epidemic. These are the last two stanzas.

The town druggist had his cure
for a man or canebrake boar.
Take head bust sucked with a reed
from an old oak-charred barrel,
a pint of that, and then drink
his gin down with Epsom salts
and store bluing. Some favored
that drink and others did not.

But no one dared swallow ice,
that was death in an instant.
So all the blistered summer
we watched each day how death came
with his black hearse and black team
while we spread out our dry hands
and there wasn't any wind
plucking at the corn tassels.

The poems in *Rivers into Islands* had capital letters and traditional punctuation, but in later poems I abandoned this practice, as did

105

many poets during the 1960's. If you use all lower case letters and no punctuation, you have to listen for the sound and the sense and line it out so the reader can hear it too. I've kept to that style ever since.

When I think back on my time in East St. Louis, I remember how rich and productive the place was and how many good friends from there are still in the deep recesses of my memory.

John Knoepfle

My Mother Dies

During my first year teaching in East St. Louis, my mother's health failed rapidly. The cancer had returned. When we came back to Cincinnati for Christmas, Mom was bedridden but delighted to see us and John Michael, now a healthy three month old. Peggy's father was still in Burma, but the rest of her family – her mother, Jim, Elinor and Molly and Jim's friends Rudolf and Carlos – were living on Inverness Place just off Madison Road. Much to Peggy's relief and satisfaction, John Michael had tripled his birth weight. His two grandmothers proudly hefted their plump grandson. The houses of both families were crowded with friends. It was a good time that Christmas.

Peggy brought John Michael to Cincinnati in March so that Mom could see him again. Later in the spring Rudy visited and gave her the last rites. Her voice on the phone was happy. "I'm better," she told us.

By August, Mom was hospitalized. We came home in time to be with her when she died. I was the only one keeping watch with her at that moment. Her lips were parched, and one of the hospital sisters brought her a lemon concoction to relieve that, and we shared a long silence. Then she breathed her last.

> *my mother*
> *waiting for her death*
> *said nothing*
> *but he knew her*
> *and he malingered*

until she had no strength
or she would have fought him

Mom was always worried about how she would look at her wake. Much to the distress of myself and my brothers, she would talk about this while we were eating our mashed potatoes, fretting over whether she should have an expression of pious hope or serene contentment. The last time she did this, my tape recorder happened to be on. After she was through, I called my brothers in and we listened to what she had to say. She never talked about it again. I don't know if it was because she was embarrassed by the tape or because she felt her wishes were now permanently on record. In any case, Mr. Sullivan, the undertaker, took years of worry from her features.

Peggy, who is more objective than I about Mom's funeral soliloquy, said after hearing the tape for the first time that I obviously had inherited my poetic talent from my mother. And it is true that I paid her the compliment of stealing her lines about "pious hope or serene contentment." They appear in a poem called "The Four Morticians," written after I had journeyed to Montgomery in the 1960's.

Cora Grundy came to the gathering at our house after my mother's funeral, as did my mother's oldest friend, Nelly Terhune. They were the last members of that generation that I knew from my boyhood – the women who sat at my mother's kitchen table. Cora sharing lunch and stories. Minta Burke, Nelly Terhune, Alice Kavaney in the evening, sometimes sharing a brew and always – stories.

That evening we brought out my father's mahogany box that held the rubber poker chips. I don't have any idea why this happened, but we stacked the chips one on one until they were very high. John Michael, who was ten months old by then, was watching. He saw the stack slowly rise until it was almost as tall as he was. Then he took the last chip from the box and while we held our breaths, carefully placed it on top of the stack without knocking it over.

Raising a Family in Edwardsville

After my mother's death, we were able to put a down payment on a house in Edwardsville with a small legacy from her will. Located on Rose Avenue, our new home was on a grassy, downward sloping hill four miles from the site of the proposed SIU Edwardsville campus. We anticipated that it would be a good place to be once the campus was built.

It seemed that we were settling down and our life was becoming more secure, but we soon learned that there were some things we could not control. That Christmas Eve, Peggy suffered a miscarriage. We were at the house of some friends. I remember driving off at top speed into the night with Peggy lying in the back seat, only to discover I was going in the wrong direction. I made a U turn, and we arrived at St. Mary's Hospital in Highland in record time. But this was Peggy's second miscarriage. We were beginning to wonder if we would be able to have any more children.

Although we had good friends in Edwardsville, we also found that people had odd stereotypes of poets and academics. On one occasion, I gave a dinner reading for a group of local businessmen. They found it amusing when I was introduced as a poet. I felt their contempt – so I read "Prodigal" and hit three lines near the end of the poem with everything I had:

> *And he will kneel to men*
> *Because he was a man,*
> *And they will let him eat with swine.*

They got the message, and the reading turned out all right.

English teachers were sometimes seen as harmless eccentrics rightfully consigned to a marginal position in the scheme of things. When I told a newly hired university administrator that I had been teaching in East St. Louis for four years, he replied, "You've been here longer, but I bet I'm making more money."

Meanwhile, important events were taking place in Peggy's family. Her parents and her sisters, Elinor and Molly, had returned from Adana, Turkey, where her father had completed work on an engineering project. That fall Elinor was married to John Petuskey, a captain in the U.S. Air Force. They had met when she was working at İncirlik Air Force Base where he was stationed. John and Elinor were moving to Offutt Air Force Base in Omaha, and Peggy's parents were about to leave for Ethiopia where her father had another engineering assignment.

So Peggy's youngest sister, Molly, came to live with us. She would go to Edwardsville High School and help take care of John Michael. This proved to be a godsend because Peggy was having another difficult pregnancy and needed total bed rest. Since I was gone from early morning until late at night, Molly's help when she came home from school was essential. During the day we were able to hire a young woman to come in during school hours – she told Peggy about a new dance called the twist – but full-time care would have been impossible.

We were convinced our second child would be a Democrat because the baby jumped in the womb the night John Kennedy was elected. On April 5, 1961, I drove again at top speed to St. Mary's Hospital. Molly – Mary Catherine – Knoepfle was born shortly after we arrived. She is the fifth in a long line of Molly's on the Irish side of Peggy's family. Our granddaughter, Molly Renee is the sixth. She is David and Robin's middle child, sister to Austin and to Hannah.

Life at 13 Rose Avenue was a bit chaotic. I learned early to work on poems and papers while John Michael and his friend Mark rode their tricycles around the dining room table. Peggy's sister was soon busy with a science project that involved radioactive isotopes, which we received oddly enough through the mail. Although they were said to be the "non-dangerous" kind, we lived in fear of losing track of them, and once Peggy thought she had left them in the bathtub, dooming us all.

Even our pets were out of control. We had gotten a cat whom we named Ramos after a Renaissance rhetorician. This cat was subject to fits. A large hole in the bathroom wall, closed off with two planks, marked the place where I had rescued Ramos from behind the woodwork. Some friends gave us a beautiful cocker spaniel named Rembie, short for Rembrandt. Rembie could climb any fence and often did so in order to chase cars. He was so uncontrollable that we had to return him to his original owners to save him from being killed by a car or an irate neighbor. Perhaps we had bad luck with our pets because we gave them names they could not live up to. Years later, we would have two wonderful dogs named Mooch and Joe. Mooch lived to be nineteen and Joe seventeen.

At the end of the school year, I had completed my residency at St. Louis University. Enjoying some free time, I used to sit on the front porch swing with my new daughter. This irritated our neighbor across the street. He would roll his car window down and ask me when was I going to get a real job?

Peggy's sister Molly had also completed a year at Edwardsville High School. She went on to Omaha to help Elinor, who was expecting a baby in July. In the fall, Molly joined her parents in Addis Ababa. She studied at the university there and walked in the garden where Emperor Haile Selassie kept his lions. We have a photograph of her in some distress when one of these lions yawned and rolled up against her shoulder.

Friends and Mentors

When we first met in 1958, the poet Peter Simpson was a graduate student at St. Louis University. He had been a student at Notre Dame and knew John Logan – it may have been Logan who brought us together. Pete and I became cohorts.

The next year he was hired at the residence center as an instructor, so now there were two poets teaching in East St. Louis. Pete encouraged a lively scene there. He put on poetry festivals – they were coming into vogue then because the Beats had made such a big impact. He also founded a student magazine called the *Penny Broadside*, I think. He brought writers in. I remember Logan read there once.

Peggy and I often visited Pete and his wife Helen. In a poem called "Street Sounds," I tried to capture a moment at the Simpson's apartment in south St. Louis.

> *Charcoal cracks in the burner*
> *where Kate and John and Carrie*
> *dream at noon to a music box*
> *that trails a firefly grace,*
> *touching a light to their slender*
> > *needs.*

One summer night in 1958, Peggy was reading a copy of *Poetry* and found a poem that she liked. "It has a gas station in it!" she told me. It was one of Robert Bly's "Ascension of J. P. Morgan" poems. Peggy liked the politics and the gas station. I liked the quality of the light and a kind of dark lonesomeness in it. I wrote to Robert telling him how much I enjoyed the poem. He sent a gracious reply and with it copies of his magazine, *The Fifties*.

I learned then that he had been translating the work of the Peruvian poet, Cesar Vallejo. As it happened, we had also been translating Vallejo. Peggy had brought a copy of the Argentine edition of his poems when she came back from Peru. She had lined out some literal translations, and I had shaped them. I sent Robert some of these poems. He and James Wright, who was working with Robert at the time, decided that they liked them, and so they added some of my translations to the book they were working on: *Twenty Poems of Cesar Vallejo*. Here are some lines from my version of Vallejo's poem, "Agape."

This afternoon everyone, everyone goes by
without asking or begging me anything.
And I do not know what it is they forget, and it is
heavy in my hands like something stolen.

I have come to the door, and I want to shout at
everyone:
– If you miss something, here it is!

This story has a coda. Jim and I wrote the two prefaces to *Twenty Poems*. Mine was influenced by the preface in the Argentine edition, which referred to Vallejo's mestizo heritage. Peggy had translated this for me and added a few memories she had of neighborhoods in Lima and the indigenous music that was played there.

The novelist and poet Jimmy Welch would tell me later that those references to the "lonesome barrios" of Lima helped him see that he could write about the experience of Native Americans in U.S. cities.

Robert and I kept in touch and sometime later – 1959 or 1960, I think – John Logan, Pete Simpson and myself drove to Madison, Minnesota, to visit Robert and his wife Carol on their farm. We drove north for hours and then turned west toward Madison, and Pete roared us past the Sacred Heart Police Station in Sacred Heart, Minnesota, at 95 miles an hour. There we were: three midwestern poets, three Catholic poets. Oh, the silence was profound in that car. Worried about Pete's driving, I took over the wheel. Pete and Logan spent the rest of the trip trying to see who could come up with the best Sacred Heart Police Station poem.

We got to Robert's farm, and we exchanged cheerful greetings and back thumpings and there was some bourbon, I think, and the farmhouse kitchen was suffused in my memory with that same yellow light that Robert had flooded the gas station with in his poem. Jim Wright was there also. Both of us had grown up in the Ohio River valley, and we shared some common interests.

Later, when we lived in University City, Missouri, Robert would come to stay with us for a few days, while he was doing a reading at St. Louis University. He did me a great favor then. He looked over my manuscript for *Rivers into Islands* and applied the same critique that he and Donald Hall and other friends used when they went over each other's poems. "What are you trying to say here?" is the question Robert kept asking. He told me, "Each time you think the next poem will get through, but it doesn't."

He also cautioned me against being nostalgic. Too many of my river poems, he said, were laments for a past that is gone. I have to admit he was right.

On another occasion, Pete and I established a handsome though short-lived literary magazine called *Deep Channel Packet*. We printed it off the mimeograph machine of the Washington University Athletic Department where Pete's sister worked as a secretary. I remember one evening some of the coaches came by and stopped to watch our progress and comment on our poems. We took turns editing. I did the second and last edition.

In the first issue, the lead essay, "*Burnt Norton* in St. Louis," was contributed by one of our professors, Walter J. Ong, S.J. He noted that when T. S. Elliot was growing up, he lived in a house adjoining Mary Institute, a private school for girls. Ong suggested that the formal garden in "*Burnt Norton*" might have been inspired in part by a formal garden at the school.

Father Ong was internationally known for his groundbreaking books on language and rhetoric. What I learned in his classes confirmed my interest in oral history and the spoken word. He encouraged my attempts to come to terms with the real language my students were writing in East St. Louis and to teach them well.

He was also on the advisory board for the Voice Project, an experimental seminar chaired by the novelist John Hawkes at Stanford University. Because of my experiences teaching in East St. Louis, I was invited to Stanford as a consultant for the project.

I remember a seminar where we listened over and over to a tape of three small boys telling a little girl how they were going to kill an elephant. They sounded aggressive, but as it turned out, the boys knew that the girl was sick and were telling this story as a way of supporting her and protecting her. The boys did not know that the girl was dying.

The head of the English program at St. Louis University was Father Maurice McNamee, famous for his dry wit and his wide-ranging interest in art. One of his books, *Honor and the Epic Hero*, was pirated by every teacher I knew because it was so useful in explaining under-achievers, over-achievers and unassailable heroes. It also worked for characters in novels and for real people.

These two scholars, Father Ong and Father MacNamee, are legendary in the history of St. Louis University. They were also men of compassion and understanding. A year after I'd completed my coursework and left their classrooms, they came to help me preside over the burial of our third child, James Girard, who did not survive the day of his birth. Peggy, who had spent many weeks in the hospital before his birth, never saw him and was still in the hospital when I arranged his burial in a plot called "Babyland" in Calvary Cemetery in St. Louis.

John Knoepfle

For a child who lived six hours

After the morning there was no noon
and now I leave your little white box
among the elms here. I give you back
with the harsh wind, howling
of the moonstruck dog, sleet,
rain, hail, the snow, the summer thunder,
wings that ruffle the air,
shapes of shadows in the deep waters.

My advisor, Professor William C. McAvoy, was a Shakespeare bibliographer. Perhaps because he had been a student of my brother Rudy at St. Ignatius High School in Cleveland, McAvoy understood that I was, indeed, older than the other graduate students. He agreed with my suggestion that I do my dissertation on the plays of Marlowe rather than Shakespeare because Marlowe had written far fewer plays. He encouraged me to finish *Formulas for Praise in the Dramas of Christopher Marlowe* on schedule. And I did.

To say that I was writing on schedule is no exaggeration. My timeline coincided with the birth of two more sons. When David was born on May 15, 1964, I would sometimes – to get a little peace and quiet – drive over to Heman Park in University City with my books and papers and get some studying done in the car. Christopher was born on July 30, 1965. On July 29, Peggy and I working far into the night, completed the final edit of the dissertation. These two small sons took over the solarium that had been my study. Lacking a place to read, I spent many hours with John, Molly, David and Chris, watching Roger Ramjet and Bullwinkle on our black and white television set in the dining room.

But to return to my friends and mentors at the residence center and the graduate school – without their friendship, I would have given up long ago. They played a big part in my life then and in the years to come and deeply influenced the way I thought and wrote.

John Knoepfle

Edged Out

My schedule the year I got my residency at
St. Louis U. was demanding. I drove to St. Louis
in the early morning and spent the day taking
graduate English classes. I then taught for three
hours at the residence center in the evenings,
returning to our house in Edwardsville, usually
by the road below the bluffs, at about eleven at
night. I took as my model the gunnery officer on
the cruiser Houston when it steamed between
two Japanese columns. He'd fire to port and
then yell, "Set 'em up in the other alley," and
fire to starboard.

That spring the vice president of Southern
Illinois University Carbondale came to visit the
residence centers and speak to small groups of
faculty to find out what we were doing and how
we felt about things. When I told him about my
studies and my teaching hours and the fact that
the translations I had done with James Wright
and Robert Bly were on the way to being pub-
lished, his response surprised me. He said that
at Carbondale a teacher going back to get a doc-
torate was never required to teach a full load
and that, in view of the fact that I'd been teach-
ing four years, I should now be an assistant pro-
fessor. He advised me to speak to my program
director. There was nothing secret about this. It
was just something that came up in an open
session with other faculty present. I was over-
joyed and eager to share this information.

I let the head of the English program know
what the vice president had said, and to my
astonishment the head of the program accused

me of going behind his back. He refused my request for the promotion, and he refused to cut my hours. When the dean backed his decision, I knew that my time at the East St. Louis residence center was up. At the end of the spring semester I would be once again out of a job, but this time with a wife and two children depending on me for their support.

It happened that the professor who was teaching Honors English at St. Louis University High School had died that spring. When Father McNamee learned of my situation, he recommended me as a replacement. I accepted, but meanwhile we had to get through the summer. I cashed in my share of the SIU retirement plan.

I did meet with the dean one more time before I left. He said, "Mr. Knoepfle, you have to learn to play the game according to the rules."

I said, "If you're a man, you change the rules." It didn't do me any good, of course, but I got some satisfaction out of it.

I should add that within the next year, Pete was also eased out of East St. Louis. A few years later he returned to what was now SIU-Edwardsville, as a special assistant to university president John Rendleman. One of the first things Pete did was to look up his records where he found he was listed as a "known Democrat."

When I left East St. Louis, I left a number of fellow teachers who were steadfast friends. One of them was Milton Byrd, who had been brought in to head up the program. I met him years later at an MLA conference where he introduced me as "one of the great comp teachers." I have also been good friends with the poet Eugene Redmond. He has created a wonderful, multi-media, multicultural literary scene in East St. Louis and at SIU-Edwardsville, and is the founder of the literary magazine, *Drum Voices*. He was not a student of mine, but he attended the residence center, and over the years we have shared some good times at poetry readings and conferences. And I have been invited to the Edwardsville campus several times to give readings and visit classes.

761 Heman Avenue

I began teaching at St. Louis University High School in September, 1961. You have to remember what was in the local newspapers in those days. If an atomic bomb fell on Kansas City, the prevailing winds would wipe out St. Louis and most of southern Illinois. It was in this context that I was teaching these young boys and raising my own children. Atomic disquiet began to seep into my poems and those of many other poets. The west wind in a poem I wrote about football practice at the high school is the prevailing wind from Kansas City, the wind that can carry the fallout.

October Scrimmage

Below the office window
players stretch their cleats
over sweat socks. They wear
promethean shoulder pads
this ancient afternoon, and I
can hear the murmur of their chatter
magnified down classroom brick
from where I crouch
within my cage of glass.
The team they play for
is famous in this town, and they
are all heroes. On the field
the scrimmage roars in dust
the wind whirls from the west
away, always from the west,
away, and the sun there

124

wrinkles a shadow line of oak
against the school wall
in back of the boys who spit
on their hands and roll laces
to thread impossible eyes.

In December, we rented a two-bedroom apartment with a solarium on Heman Avenue in University City. For Peggy, it was like returning home. When she had finished the eighth grade in Anderson Ranch Dam, Idaho, her parents had sent her to live with her aunt and uncle and her cousin Doug in University City so that she could go to high school there. She had friends in the area, and they became friends of mine.

The landlord of our new apartment lived across the hall from us. He was a survivor of the Warsaw Ghetto. His father had taken him to the barbed wire fence at the edge of the ghetto, had cut the wire and told him to leave and to run as fast as he could. He had done so, joined a partisan group and survived the war. His mother-in-law came to visit us the day we moved in. She looked around our living room at the bookcases and boxes of books and said with pleasure, "Oh, you are a scholar."

That was our welcome to University City – we have never forgotten the joy and relief we felt on hearing those words. Burdens we didn't know we were carrying fell from our shoulders.

From our living room window we could see Aldine Fisher's study lit up late at night just like mine. He was a young professor of philosophy at St. Louis University. The novelist and short story writer Stanley Elkin lived right up the street

125

from Aldine's and Rosemary Fisher's apartment. Jim and Carolyn Scott, soon to become dear friends, lived a couple of blocks east on Interdrive. Jim taught in the St. Louis University English Department, where his interest in cinema led him to teach it and then to become a writer and director of television documentaries. Carolyn would brilliantly teach liberal arts studies at Lindenwood College. Down the street from the Scotts lived two young poets, Donald Finkel and his wife Constance Urdang. And not far away on Teasdale Avenue, the poet Mona Van Dyne and her husband, Jarvis Thurston, a creative writing teacher and editor at nearby Washington University, had a welcoming house for area artists and writers.

Our friend Norman Hinton and his wife Jo Ann and their four children lived over on Melrose Avenue. Peggy would later teach Susie their eldest in Sunday school at All Saints Church. Norm, a medievalist at St. Louis University, played the guitar at sing along parties at our house. Ted Haddin was another St. Louis University colleague. Poet, concert violinist, Thoreau scholar, Ted had also been a cook for the crew of a Great Lakes ore boat.

Peggy and I felt that at last we had come to a place where we belonged.

Epilogue

Living in University City would be the noontide of my life and Peggy's. As I recounted earlier, James Girard, David and Christopher were all born during our time there – James not surviving his first day. John, Molly, David and Chris would spend childhood years as students at Delmar Harvard. Peggy was at Abe Pultman's delicatessen one day with our son David when he was still a toddler. The old men who liked to lounge there in their long overcoats and fedora hats admired him and asked Peggy his name. When she told them, they gathered around him and gave him a blessing.

Our children would explore the city parks and play baseball on diamonds there. And during the 1963 heat wave, our family would be standing shoulder to shoulder with the entire population, it seemed, of University City in the cool water of our enormous community swimming pool in Heman Park.

The University of Chicago Press, as I noted before, would publish *Rivers into Islands*, and I would work through my doctorate. In the process I would argue, in addition to the matter of the dissertation, that there is a seven-step movement toward despair in Marlowe's *Faustus*, which parallels an analysis of despair in one of Bishop John Fisher's sermons on the penitential psalms. These steps are also definitive in *Macbeth*, but at the time I did not catch Shakespeare's greater complexity. The steps are also in Heywood's play, *A Woman Killed with Kindness*, but not the seventh, of course.

I would continue to teach wherever I could to support my growing family. I would be four years as an assistant professor at Maryville College and at the same time would log in three years with the Great Books at Washington University's Evening College, while occupying summers at the Mark Twain Summer Institute. There would also be stints at Webster College and at St. Louis University in specialized offerings. Then I would be hired to head the creative writing program in the St. Louis University English Department. In one golden year, I was awarded a grant from the Rockefeller Foundation, and the university made up the difference between the grant and my salary. This plus eight readings in colleges across the country and site visits to eight Upward Bound projects for the Office of Economic Opportunity would provide the down payment needed to move our family from our Heman Avenue apartment to the house on 732 Trinity in University Heights, close to the fire station and the stone lions guarding the steps to City Hall.

a good thaw and I
walking on delmar boulevard
it is ten miles to the river
low billows of white cloud
tell me where it is and here
the flat wall of the temple
the orthodox church with its
copper dome shaggy with snow
the curious masonic facade and these
gates paired with lions
top heavy and leaning

One of my most popular University City poems was "I know the names of all the dogs in my neighborhood." There were fifty-three in all, among them our dog Mooch, and Don and Connie Finkel's dog Binker. Falafel, the Rabbi's delinquent dog, lived up the street and was father to Mooch's second litter of puppies. The last dog in the poem was Lumpi Von Eichenruh. He belonged to Clarence and Jean Miller – Clarence a colleague at St. Louis University, a Thomas More scholar and editor.

We would spend a summer in upstate New York when I taught in the session at SUNY-Buffalo. Good in the memory, a tribe of scholars, poets, critics and actors in the session that year. I took Jim Wright to the university and back weekdays. He had no mechanical skills and didn't drive. We had much in common, a mutual interest in and knowledge of the Ohio River Valley. That was the summer a U.S. Astronaut took a small step for himself on the moon and a great step for mankind.

In those restive days in the 1960's, I would be called out of myself as so many were. I went on one occasion to the South on a bus out of St. Louis, many of my fellow passengers having more experience than I did with civil protest. When the bus traveled the highway into Birmingham, the driver pointed out what fine houses black people were living in. He simply did not see the bombed out church on the other side of the road. I would visit in Montgomery the short time I was there, speak with a quiet woman in her ranch house living room who would tell me that she was reprimanded because she lost control in her class, but she said that when those boys from Michigan came in singing their freedom songs, she was crying. Her daughter, sitting unresponsive on the living room rug, had been kicked in the head by one of the horses in Sheriff Clark's posse.

I would owe a lot to Paul Hanlon, at the time teaching Sociology at St. Louis University and deeply involved in the Civil Rights Movement. His wife, Ella Jo, was both friend and mentor to Peggy. I would meet John Howard Griffin, author of *Black Like Me*, over coffee one morning in the Hanlon kitchen. Paul would organize the massive demonstration that occurred in St. Louis after the assassination of Dr. Martin Luther King, Jr.

In the months that followed, I would make my last visit for Upward Bound, this time to Holly Springs, Mississippi, and then on to Alcorn A & M in Lorman, and then east across the South to Savannah, Georgia. What to say. It was so quiet everywhere, everyone stunned to silence by the deaths of King and Robert Kennedy. But I would be challenged on another count in Savannah. A young man asked me if I was willing to go a hundred percent. I asked him if he was willing to die for my children. When he said no, I told him to take any percent he could get. And suddenly people were smiling around me, and I heard someone say, "Why, yes, why should we expect a hundred percent from Matilda the way she was brought up?" I believe that many in the room were able to shift an uncomfortable burden that afternoon.

In those years our family would become part of a congregation that celebrated Sunday Mass in the basement of St. Louis University's not-yet-renovated College Church. We were enthusiastic singers of hymns like "If I Had a Hammer" and "They'll Know We are Christians by our Love." We would speak from the altar our concerns about what was happening in our families and in our country – and in Viet Nam.

Peggy and I protested the war, as did Peggy's parents and her sister Molly, even as we prayed for Peggy's brother Jim, a Captain in the Marines in Chu Lai and Da Nang and her sister Elinor's husband John Petuskey, a Colonel in the Air Force in Saigon. Peggy remembers conflicting emotions and perceptions on every front, an inability to feel totally a part of any political program. There were letters, conversations – and silences. The family would hold together.

Visiting Viet Nam just this last year, Peggy's sister Elinor would find in the intense emotional experience evoked by that visit of the pain and waste of war just how much she had kept pent up in her day-by-day effort to keep herself together and care for the children. It was a time of strained hope and intense anguish.

> *where am I in all this yesterday*
> *the fig tree would not bloom*
>
> *and now the elections*
> *hook the bodies of officials*
> *and drag them up*
> *from vats of formaldehyde*

the priest is lonely

he uncovers his chalice
for a drop of rain

We would feel grief and anger when St. Louis's Cardinal John Carberry closed down the Lower College Church. And people from all over the city would join our protest that filled the St. Louis University quad on a bright and sad spring morning.

Peggy and I would remain in the larger Church, determined not to relinquish what we felt was ours. Our friends, Jim and Carolyn Scott would move on, focusing their spiritual energies on the arts and on the renewal of University City's decaying Delmar strip. And that is how Cardinal Carberry may be said to have contributed in a small way to the restoration of the Tivoli Theater.

Our family would discover the Ozarks – all of us awed by our first sight of an Ozark spring:

blue coin of earth generous in that
green hickory light shafting
through elm and the smell of cedar . . . .

And the Johnson Shut-ins. Even Peggy, always remembering her Rocky Mountain childhood, would be impressed.

we climb down
working through rapids
the wet rock slippery
small falls catching us

John Knoepfle

helpless into pools
laughing
although you sense
deep openings in crevices and
terror a little

On one memorable afternoon, 14-year-old John Michael would hike up the cliff that overlooks the deep pool at the foot of the Shut-ins and jump 35 feet into its depths, emerging laughing in a spray of white foam. He would be followed by eleven-year-old Molly, who then climbed back up the cliff and did it again to show what a girl can do and prove the first time wasn't a fluke.

The Shut-ins would be magnets for our son Chris decades later when he would pause in his travels to visit them. Chris saw the Shut-ins not long before the disaster of December 2005 when the Tam Sauk dam broke and a wall of water and silt buried the porphyry formations. Nine months later, Peggy and I would walk with Molly and our granddaughter Emily along trails skirting a shut-down river and would stand with pride and trepidation on the edge of the very cliff Molly had jumped from. Emily's suggestion that she might like to do the same someday evoked an ambiguous response from her mother.

And one morning on Trinity Avenue in University City, Howard Schwartz would walk over to our house with Charles Simic to pay a visit. They would admire the print I had from Upward Bound with its quote from Tolstoy. And then I would drive them to Clayton so that Simic could buy a fire truck for his daughter.

This is good place to stop writing my short autobiography, don't you think?

I have to say that in 1972, our family would move back to Illinois where I would join the faculty at Sangamon State University, then known as the Berkeley of the Midwest. The town we would live in for the next thirty years was Auburn, Illinois. Twenty miles south and west of Springfield, it was named after Oliver Goldsmith's "loveliest village on the plain."

We would settle in a house built in 1872 on property carved from a Van Buren land grant, an odd choice for an urban family such as ours. But we would make many friends there and become one of Auburn's football dynasty families with three all-conference sons – and a daughter with lifelong friends whom she hastens to visit whenever she comes back from Anchorage. I would write *Poems from the Sangamon* there and *Dim Tales*, books shaped by craft and scholarship but also by my life in Auburn. I would come to say: "For a poet, I am in a very good place."

> *this house is old*
> *it has known kindred*
> *and candles at the suppers*
> *and some who spoke in those tall lights*
> *far away in their truth*
> *it has known many children I think*
> *with their soft lazy friends*
> *the windowsill cats*
> *a few dogs good for nothing*
> *but a journey with tobias*
> *this house is kindly*
> *it will not go down easy*

John Knoepfle

And yet during the process of writing this book, I have realized that by 1961 when I cross- ed the river to teach and raise my family in St. Louis, my life was already set in its course by the experiences, people and places I talk about in these pages. I was particularly moved when I remembered the many efforts of my friends and school mates in Cincinnati to find employment and a place in the world for me during my troubled young manhood.

Sources for Poems Cited

"there was the candle christmas eve," from
  "Lines for my Mother," *Prayer Against Famine
  And Other Irish Poems*, BkMk Press, 20.
"I carried his ashes," from "Lines for my
  Grandfather," *Rivers into Islands*, The
  University of Chicago Press, 46.
"Now a Dark Matter," from "Sister Miriam's
  Poem," *Illinois Times*, April 8, 2004.
"Marquette in Winter Camp, Chicago River,
  1675," *Poems from the Sangamon*, University
  of Illinois Press, 7.
"Those massive locomotives," from "Diesel,"
  Rivers into Islands, 9.
"calling us out of ourselves," from "Gandiji," *The
  Chinkapin Oak*, Rosehill Press, 62.
"Dropping one by one her silver combs," from
  "On a Fall Night," *The Yale Review*, Autumn,
  1953.
"Down Solomon," *Rivers into Islands*, 42.
"Night of Stars and Flowers," *Rivers into Islands*,
  14.
"O Mystery, who am I?" from *A Christmas
  Oratorio*, *The Xavier Athenaeum*, 1947.
"he is a pretty good cat," *Dogs and Cats and Things
  Like That*," McGraw-Hill Book Company,
  #4.
"Like some ungainly bird this banjo," *Rivers into
  Islands, 3. The Yale Review*, 117.
"Church of Rose of Lima, Cincinnati," *Rivers
  into Islands*, 20.
"near the rosebud the santee said," *A Gathering
  of Voices*, Scrimshaw Editions, Rook Press,
  18.
"Heroin," *Prayer Against Famine and other Irish
  Poems*, 23.

"Why is it pain holds us something less?" from
    "Sparrows," *Fleur de Lis*, St. Louis University,
    1960.
"love is like a bowl," *A Gathering of Voices*, 21.
"Coal sells a bushel a week," from "East St.
    Louis," *Rivers into Islands*, 5.
"Above the oil refinery," from "Night Fire," *Rivers
    into Islands*, 29.
"The town druggist had his cure," from "Country
    Sweat," *Rivers into Islands*, 6.
"my mother," *A Gathering of Voices*, 22.
"pious hope or serene contentment," "The Four
    Morticians," *Intricate Land*, 53.
"Prodigal," *Western Humanities Review*, Winter,
    1960.
"*Charcoal cracks in the burner*," from "Street
    Sounds," *Rivers into Islands*, 10.
"This afternoon everyone," from "Agape," *Twenty
    Poems of Cesar Vallejo*, chosen and translated
    by John Knoepfle, James Wright and Robert
    Bly, 25.
"For a child who lived six hours," *Rivers into
    Islands*, 41.
"October scrimmage," *Rivers into Islands*, 25.
"a good thaw," from "His Day the Baptist,"
    Selected Poems, 78.
"where am I," *Thinking of Offerings: Poems 1970-
    1973*, Juniper Press, 17.
"Ozark Spring," from "From a Missouri Land
    Grant," *Selected Poems*, 55.
"Shut Ins," from "From a Missouri Land Grant,"
    Selected Poems, 55-56.
"this house is old," *Selected Poems*, 100.

John Knoepfle

Biography

For six decades, John Knoepfle has been writing poems, and he's still going strong. Knoepfle writes love poems, among the best we have, of the joys, loneliness, danger and the infinite transformations of marriage. He writes narrative poems, surreal, sardonic and magical about astronauts on the moon or an angry farmer and a prophetic owl. He recovers the stories of folks who never made it into the history books. Always he has a respect for the spoken word and lays his lines out on the page so that you too can hear it. And a spiritual force runs through his books like the slow and powerful rivers of the Midwest he inhabits. Both moving and humorous, Knoepfle's autobiography shows us how by hard work and lucky accident he came to be the poet he is.

Books from Pearn and Associates, Inc.

I Look Around For My Life,
Autobiography
By John Knoepfle

Goulash and Picking Pickles,
Autobiography
By Louise Mae Hoffmann

The U Book,
Photos, Poems and Journal Notes from India
By Nathan Preston Pierce

Ikaria: A Love Odyssey on a Greek Island
Creative Nonfiction
By Anita Sullivan

Another Chance,
Fiction
By Joe Naiman

Point Guard,
Fiction
By Victor Pearn

Books may be ordered through amazon.com, barnesandnoble.com, your local bookstore, (Ingram Books) you may order for libraries through Baker and Taylor, and books may be ordered directly from the publisher at:
happypoet@hotmail.com.

Printed in the United States
106958LV00004B/8/P